To Bill,

Thank you for showing us your beautiful county.

From Jo & Jack.

GROVE HOUSE

FEB. 2002.

BYGONE Harrogate

Harrogate Advertiser

BYGONE
Harrogate

Malcolm Neesam

The Breedon Books
Publishing Company
Derby

First published in Great Britain by
The Breedon Books Publishing Company Limited
Breedon House, 44 Friar Gate, Derby, DE1 1DA.
1999

**Published 1999, during the Millennial Mayoralty of
Councillor George Crowther OBE, Mayor of Harrogate
County Councillor Joan M. Crowther, Mayoress of Harrogate**

ISBN 1 85983 155 9

Printed and bound by Butler & Tanner Ltd., Selwood Printing Works,
Caxton Road, Frome, Somerset.

Colour separations and jacket printing by GreenShires Ltd, Leicester.

— Contents —

Dedicated to my friend
and fellow historian
Ann London

Introduction

MALCOLM NEESAM'S *Bygone Harrogate* column is one of the *Harrogate Advertiser's* most popular weekly features, and there have been repeated requests from readers for them to be issued in more permanent form. This book includes the majority of the *Bygone Harrogate* articles published in the *Harrogate Advertiser* from 1996 to Easter 1999, as well as a selection of the author's longer articles, so that the volume provides readers with a representative selection of Malcolm Neesam's popular historical writing. In addition, the book includes a considerable number of photographs never previously reproduced in either books or newspapers, and which add new perspective to the reader's awareness of how Harrogate once appeared. The author has edited and amended each article, to take account of developments since the original date of publication.

Malcolm Neesam is the first to acknowledge, with gratitude, the important role of *Harrogate Advertiser* readers in supplying many of the photographs which form such a significant aspect of *Bygone Harrogate* articles. The author has, for the purposes of brevity and avoidance of repetition, abandoned the habit of acknowledging donors within the body of each article, adopting rather the reference 'supplied by...' at the end of each text. The author has also purchased copies of many photographs, originally supplied by readers, from booksellers, postcard fairs and private dealers. To all readers who lent photographs to Malcolm Neesam, regardless of whether or not they are named in this book, the author expresses his sincerest thanks. Special mention must be made to the generosity of four *Harrogate Advertiser* readers, who have repeatedly allowed the author access to their splendid collections: David Hird, Clifford Hopes, David Lewis and Simon Townson; without them, this book could not have appeared. The postcard views reproduced with a single line of caption have been supplied by Clifford Hopes and David Lewis, to whom the author again extends sincere thanks.

Parliament Street

Parliament Street is seen here in about 1906. At far left is the building which collapsed so dramatically in April 1992, and which was rebuilt in 1998 to accommodate the Hogshead public house. The building served for many years as the location for Charles Walker's furnishings store and undertakers business, before they moved across the street to occupy what is now the Westminster Arcade. Next to this stands an unusual building, which survives in virtually unchanged condition, save for its attractive spiked dormer windows, removed in the major refurbishment of 1982.

This building – once known as the 'Exchange' – had been erected in 1870, and to the best of the author's knowledge was the first important retail development in the town to employ Pease's white brick, interspersed with dressed stone from Richardson's Birk Crag Quarry. Before the coming of the railways in the late 1840s, Harrogate had been built entirely of stone, and the bricks from the local brickworks were used only for unimportant rear elevations, or for internal purposes such as party walls and chimneys. After the railways however, brick came to be imported in considerable amounts, the first substantial use for them being in the building of the Central Railway Station. The 'Exchange' block came very near to being demolished between 1974 and 1982, when it was the subject of one of the town's longest conservation battles.

The card also shows, at right, Edwardian visitors enjoying the splendidly wide pavement as they pass the building now occupied by Fattorini's, which had been built by George Dawson back in 1866-68. [Supplied by Mr S. Townson]

Tom Rochford

On 3 October 1931, the *Harrogate Herald* carried news of the death of 'Old Tom' of Brunswick Cottage, West Park, at the age of 81. Thomas Rochford, known throughout the town as 'Old Tom', was the Father of the Harrogate Bath Chair men, and a familiar figure, respected by residents and visitors alike. He had been the first man to introduce Harrogate to the Coventry Cycle Chair, a means of transportation which combined the comfort of the Bath Chair with the pedal power of the bicycle, a very popular mode of

transport with visitors to the town. Tom Rochford had been credited with the introduction to Harrogate, along with his friend Gallagher, a retired Police Sergeant of Albert Terrace, with the introduction of the Bath Chair proper to Harrogate. But for the new-fangled Coventry Cycle Chair, Tom Rochford co-operated with another friend, Sylvester Medici, whose brother owned a cycle shop on Prospect Crescent. Rochford's enthusiasm for the Cycle Chair paid dividends after about 1880, as they rapidly enjoyed great demand. Contrary to later popular opinion, the cycle chairs were not used solely by the elderly or infirm, but were popular with all ages.

The photograph shows a Pedal Cycle made in Harrogate by a company called Slee's Cycle Manufactory, who operated at first from premises in Tower Street [more or less opposite to the present Tap and Spile pub], which they shared with Octavius Atkinson, and a pub called the Coach Makers Arms. Later, Slee's moved to Trafalgar Road, and it is possible that this photograph was taken at the firms Trafalgar Road premises.

Tom Rochford is listed in the Directories as a Bath Chair Man, and in the early years of the century, he appears to have lived at 90 Butler Road, Bilton. By 1918 however, he is listed as being at Brunswick Place,

West Park, which was convenient both for Medici's cycle shop, as well as for the Bath Chair men's shelter, which still stands at the top of Montpellier Hill.

The visitors who sat in Tom Rochford's pedal cycle included some of the greatest names of Edwardian England, the singer, Madam Patti, who hired 'Old Tom' to take her to see the Otter Hunts at the Nidd; Ellen Terry, Lord Londonderry, the Countess of Westmorland, the Duchess of Sutherland, and the Duchess of Devonshire. On one famous occasion, King Edward VII sat in the chair and complemented 'Old Tom' on the comfort of the seat. Another time, just after the end of the Boer War, Winston Churchill used to organise mass-outings of what he called the Harrogate Bathchair Artillery, setting out from Pier Head, and racing down Parliament Street, eventually ending up at Fountains Abbey. In later years, Tom Rochford recalled that Churchill had insisted on being at the front of the Bath Chair charge.

'Old Tom' also recalled his work for the youthful Princess Alex of Hesse, who stayed at Cathcart House on West Park, with her sister, Princess Louis of Battenberg, and her small daughter. Tom later described these outings in a newspaper article: 'I took her out every day for five weeks. I had received instructions from all the gentry in the district that I could go to any of their parks and estates, so I took the Princess to all the beauty spots I knew of. We went for miles into the country, and I shall never forget how kind and homely the Princess was. Most times we were alone, but often there was a detective riding a little way behind on a bicycle. Once the Princess looked round and said: "Who is that man following us?" and I replied: "He's a detective," at which she laughed and said it would be far more sensible to come and help me pedal the cycle chair. On the Princess's 22nd birthday, I took her and her sister and the little Princess to Plompton Rocks for a picnic. It was a wonderful day. The sun shone all the time and everybody was so happy. They took lunch and tea baskets, and it was good to hear them laughing among the rocks. Then the Princess told me she was leaving Harrogate. She gave me a photograph and I said I supposed I should never see her again, at which she replied that she might well come back.'

Shortly after this, the Princess married the Tsar of Russia, and was murdered by the Bolsheviks in 1918. It is tempting to speculate if, in her final anguished hours, the Tsarina recalled those far away golden days in Harrogate, with outings in Old Tom Rochford's pedal cycle.

Prospect Place

This fine view of the Prospect Hotel and Gardens, which dates from the early years of the century appears to have been taken from Cambridge Crescent, looking due south as far as the Belvédère on Victoria Avenue, and must have been just the sort of view which would impress potential visitors with the order and spaciousness of Harrogate. The Prospect Hotel is seen here without its additional top storey, which was added in 1936 by way of compensation for the loss of the northern most section of the hotel which cut across James Street.

Although this alteration effected a great improvement to James Street, it resulted in the tower of the Prospect Hotel being 'submerged' by the surrounding top floor of the hotel. The spacious garden at the foot of the postcard shows the Prospect Hotel's 'amusement garden' which provided tennis courts and croquet lawns for the use of guests. It was of course swept away in 1922, when work began on the building of the war memorial. Close inspection of the card reveals the wonderfully ornate decorative iron work which once graced the front of the hotel, until it was destroyed in 1937. The restoration of this iron work by the hotel would really effect an immense improvement to this part of the townscape. Another interesting feature of this card is that the gardens along Prospect Place are still in private ownership, being divided by hedges. The formal garden of the Prospect Hotel as befitting its status as one of the town's top addresses boasts an elaborate stone balustrade, forming an elegant backdrop. The hotel is now called the Imperial. [Supplied by Mrs Rosen]

Station Square in the grip of the winter of 1912, when the town experienced quite heavy falls of snow. Two of the talking points in the town at this time were – apart from the weather – the heroic cycle ride from Harrogate to Scarborough by Mr T. W. Monkhouse, during a terrific snowstorm on 2 February, and the unpleasantness caused by Mr Lloyd George, who told Parliament that 'even Harrogate has slums'.

The weather, however, was the chief topic of conversation, and this photograph shows the efforts of the highways department to remove snow from James Street with help from the Corporation's horse and cart.

The Victoria Monument was a gift to the town from Alderman Richard Ellis, consisting of a statue of Queen Victoria by the London sculptor Webber, set beneath a gothic canopy designed by Harrogate architect, Bown. The foundation stone was laid by Mrs Ellis on 14 April 1887, and the completed monument unveiled by the Marquis of Ripon on 6 October. The pretty little gas lamps and railings, which were such an integral part of the monument's design, were destroyed in 1941, but the splendid canopy of the Station Hotel survived until about 1950, when it too succumbed to the mania for removing ornamental iron work. In the background, the roof of the buildings on Station Bridge carries an enormous advertisement for the Great Northern Railway Passenger Booking Office.

High Harrogate College

The old Dragon Hotel in High Harrogate is pictured here when it had become the seat of the High Harrogate College. The Dragon Hotel was unquestionably one of the town's great establishments, being an apex of the High Harrogate triangle, the other two being the Granby and Queen. The Dragon, in common with Harrogate's older hotels, had its origins in much smaller structures which were originally farmhouses. These farmhouses gradually grew to accommodate the visitors to the Spa, and eventually reached gargantuan proportions in Victorian times, when they were given uniform, symmetrical façades such as grace the Crown, Queen, and Old Swan Hotels.

As this photograph of *c.*1870 shows the Dragon frontage retained the evidence of its antiquity, although it had then ceased to be an hotel. In its great days, the Dragon had been popular with the military, the hard living, gambling, racing set of guests, who came to Harrogate less for the Spa and more for the wealth which the Spa attracted. The Dragon was also frequented by writers such as Lawrence Sterne, the antiquarian Thomas Pennant, Sarah, the old Duchess of Marlborough, and the colourful Colonel Thornton, who would drive into Harrogate at the head of a column of hounds, falconers, and archers, distributing largesse and good cheer to all who greeted him.

Alas, the Dragon was eclipsed by Low Harrogate in Victorian times, and converted into a school in *c.*1870. It was visited before its demolition in 1886, by the great painter Frith, who had spent his boyhood at the Dragon, and who regretted its derelict condition. Following demolition, Mornington Crescent was built on the site, and the extensive gardens and farm at the rear were developed into the Dragon estate. In this photograph, we see the boys of High Harrogate College enjoying a cricket match in the middle of Skipton Road.

Strawberry Dale Academy

The site at the corner of Strawberry Dale, redeveloped in 1996 for residential accommodation, originally provided a home for Low Harrogate's first known private school – the Strawberry Dale Academy. The photograph shows the teachers cottage at left, with the school premises at right, both properties being of 18th-century construction. The earliest reference to the school occurs in Baines 1822 *Yorkshire Directory*, which lists 'Miss Parry's Strawberry Dale Ladies' Academy'. By 1838, the establishment is known as Miss Parry's Strawberry Dale School, but it is not known whether at this time boys were admitted. Miss Parry's school was private, and of the type then known as a dame school, that is, a school run by a single woman providing an elementary education.

In 1855 the Duchy of Lancaster was approached by a Mr Heigham, who keeps a large school, for permission to build a new school on Beech Grove, but the concern of residents at the prospect of having a school built on their door steps led to the Duchy suggesting an alternative site. In 1863 the Duchy accepted William Heigham's application to transfer his Strawberry Dale School to a new building on Ripon road the present Southlands so it must be presumed that Catherine Parry had retired at some time before 1855. William Heigham, was born in 1801 and died in 1883, a much-respected member of the Harrogate community, and in August 1996 the author was privileged to meet his great-great-grandson, Mr J. H. Hawkins and his wife, visiting Harrogate from their home in Tennessee. Mr and Mrs Hawkins were fascinated to visit both Southlands and Strawberry Dale. Who would have thought that Strawberry Dale would one day feature on the itinerary of American tourists?

Kursaal frontage

The view from lower Parliament Street, flanked at left by the Royal Baths, and at right by Louis Cope's shop. The time is a midsummer's afternoon in the 1920s. People are strolling along the extra wide pavements of Parliament Street, passed by the occasional motor car. Two policemen stand in the middle of the crossing with King's and Crescent Roads, probably engaged in conversation about traffic! A temporary poster outside the Spa Rooms advertises dancing in the neighbouring Royal Hall from 9pm to 2pm.

This photograph was taken only a few years after the Council changed the Kursaal's name to that of the Royal Hall, whose frontage had been deliberately set well back behind the building line of the older Spa Rooms, in order to remove it as far as possible from

the traffic noise of Ripon Road and Parliament Street. Even in the 1890s this was proving a cause for concern. Indeed, the influential Francis Barber urged the Council to build their new 'Kursaal' at least eighty yards away from the Ripon Road building line, so that it would be sheltered from the noise of the ever increasing traffic.

Architects Robert Beale and Frank Matchem would have been horrified at the thought that the south façade of their important new building would one day be opened up to public view after the wanton demolition of the Spa Rooms in 1939. Old photographs also show that before World War One, the Kursaal and the Spa Rooms were fronted by a splendid row of beech trees, all of which have subsequently been chopped down.

Kursaal Front Garden

Photographed in about 1928, this view shows the little garden which separated the Royal Hall entrance road from the public footpath on Ripon Road. This garden had a dual purpose, in that it not only provided visitors to the Royal Hall with a delightful floral experience as they entered and left the building, but it also ensured that delivery vehicles were kept away from the pavement. The little garden was also important because it was the very first municipal flower bed to be seen by visitors driving in to Harrogate down the Ripon Road, thus emphasising Harrogate's claim to being Britain's floral capital.

However, when the frontage was vandalised in c.1970 by the erection of a vile corrugated canopy, the little garden was swept away and replaced with a mess of tar and paving flags. Immediately, the Ripon Road public footpath became a no-go area for pedestrians, who were obliged to skirt innumerable lorries, vans, and cars, which were not only a gross inconvenience to walkers, but which also spoiled the view of the Kursaal. However, in 1997 the original 1903 canopy was restored, and it is to be hoped that before too much time passes, someone will see the sense in also restoring the flower bed. [Supplied by Mr S. Townson]

Montpellier Road

Prints often contain just as much useful information as photographs, and this interesting example shows Montpellier Road at its junction with Crescent Road, some time around the year 1835. At that time, Montpellier Road was little more than a dirt track which divided the Thackwray's Crown Hotel from the field which extended eastwards as far as Parliament Street. It had developed as a convenient route from Cold Bath Lane to the roads to both Ripon and Bilton. The field had long been used to tether and graze the Thackwray's horses, until the chance discovery in 1822 of a valuable Sulphur Spring.

Mr Thackwray then erected a little pump room over the well, in the Chinese style, which can be seen at the centre of this print. The surrounding area was laid out as a pleasure garden for the Crown Hotel, to which the general public were admitted on payment of a small charge. To the immediate right of the pump room, a small octagonal structure may be seen, which could well be the present White Cottage, built c.1834 as a ticket office for the Crown Baths erected by Mr Thackwray. The tall house to the left of the Pump Room is part of Bath Terrace, a handsome Georgian development of the Thackwray's, in which Harrogate Corporations borough analyst, Arnold Woodmansey, worked for many years. To the far right may be seen a fragment of the eastern wall of the Crown Hotel, but of more interest, old St Mary's Church, with its tower, comes into view across the Stray.

Cambridge Street/ Cambridge Place

Few will remember the junction of Cambridge Street and Cambridge Place when it looked like this, before the Woolworth building was erected. During the 1830s, this was the site of the first substantial building to be erected in what later became Cambridge Street. This was the British School, which gave many of central Harrogate's children a primary education. Later in the century, the school was replaced by the premises shown here, which faced the Ebor public house across School Court, which changed its name to Cambridge Place in 1914.

Number 26 Cambridge Street was for many years occupied by Tindall's the ironmongers, who moved to Bower Road in 1921 when Woolworth's acquired the site, along with number 28, for their new Harrogate store. Woolworth's is in some respects a very interesting building, as it includes a number of decorative features which the discerning eye will recognise as being typical of the American art deco style. One of the little cottages down Cambridge Place, was once home to the last English bare-knuckle prizefighter.

Cheltenham Parade

Today, a traffic-choked thoroughfare which, rather unfairly, has to carry the bulk of the town's internal north to south traffic, Cheltenham Parade was mostly built by the great Harrogate builder James Simpson, beginning its life as a quiet residential road that linked the Victoria Park Company's Station Parade with King's Road and the adjacent Cheltenham Spa Rooms. The greater part of Cheltenham Parade consists of a substantial terrace, which began its life as residential properties, most of which were used as lodging houses for visitors to the Spa. The most pleasing aspect of Cheltenham Parade was the way that the terrace curved as it progressed up the hill, with clear separation of road, pavement, garden and building by the means of trees, a neat boundary wall with railings, and a uniform depth of frontage.

Today's appearance has been the result of several things: the post-war change from residential to commercial use, a change accelerated by the nearby Conference Centre; the loss of the railings in World War Two's salvage drive; the use of the parade in the 1969 plan for a five-phase traffic plan for Harrogate [never implemented, despite the urgings of the traffic planners] and worst of all, the chopping down of the trees. Cheltenham Parade's recent revival has been thanks to the enterprise and initiative of the business community, who against difficult odds, have succeeded in creating a thriving locality. But it would be nice to have the trees back.

This photograph of *c.*1909 shows the eastern edge of Crescent Gardens before the Shelter was built in 1910. For centuries, this land had been occupied by the rather unattractive Crescent Inn, which was one of Low Harrogate's oldest establishments. The purchase of the Inn by the Council and its subsequent demolition enabled the open land between the back of the Crown Hotel estate, and the New Victoria Baths (today the Municipal Buildings) to be laid out as a garden for the special convenience of the early morning drinkers at the Royal Pump Room. In the background may be seen Hale's Bar, and Farrah's Toffee shop and works, a building whose finely-dressed stone façade has in recent times been spoiled by the application of garrish paint. To the right may be seen Leamington Cottage, which still stands, built by the Crescent Inn to provide extra accommodation. Pedestrians walk with complete safety in the road, which was always closed to vehicular traffic before 10am.

Crescent Gardens south side

The south side of Crescent Gardens has always been bounded by Crescent Road, which linked the Old Sulphur Well and the junction of Cold Bath Road and Irongate Bridge Road [today, Cornwall Road] with the Leeds to Ripon Turnpike Road and the ancient route from Low Harrogate to Bilton. The development of this frontage was originally due to the Crown Hotel, who not only built the Crown, or Montpellier Baths, on that portion of their land between Montpellier Road and Parliament Street, but who, under the ownership of George Dawson, also built the entire length of property between Crown Place and Montpellier Road.

When the Montpellier Baths became inadequate to the needs of the visitors in the 1880s, Richard Ellis, and his successor on the Council, Charles Fortune, oversaw the planning and eventual erection of the great new Royal Baths, with its characteristic Harrogate dome.

Opened in 1897, the Royal Baths was the world's most advanced centre for hydrotherapy. Following closure of the Spa facilities in 1969, the Royal Baths went into decline, but the Council began a series of repairs and refurbishments in 1985, following the writing of a report to the Conference and Leisure Services Committee. Hundreds of thousands of pounds have been spent, and it is much to the Council's credit that the magnificent building is waterproof, electrically safe, and in general good repair, even to the point of being floodlit at night. It is therefore all the more impossible to understand why the Council allowed the entrance ramp pavements to be used as a dumping ground for cars. It was crazy to have allowed Harrogate's most important large Spa building to be defaced with heaps of metal rubbish, which were an affront to the eye, as well as a gross inconvenience to those who approached the entrance on foot.

The north side of Crescent Gardens remained an open field until the New Victoria Baths were built in 1871 by the Improvement Commissioners. Although the baths contained extensive treatment rooms for both men and women, they also included rooms for the Improvement Commissioners to meet, above the central entrance hall. When the New Victoria Baths were reconstructed to form the present Municipal Buildings in 1931, the same space became the Council Chamber, thus ensuring the continuity of a tradition which had begun in 1871. When the road in front of the New Victoria Baths was built, the Improvement Commissioners decided to retain a tree which now found itself in the middle of a highway.

This was because [1] the tree was a good tree, and [2] it would discourage speeding by conveyances. One hundred years later, and how attitudes have changed. In the 1970s the Council carved from the public gardens a nice little car park for themselves, thus ensuring that the northern boundary of Crescent Gardens would be lined with a horrible mess of scrap metal, which now spreads across the public pavement, making it impossible for pedestrians to cross the footpath which leads from the road to the Shelter. As there is a perfectly suitable car park a few minutes walk away in Union Street, it is absolutely indefensible for the despoilation of Crescent Gardens to continue.

Grand Hotel and Valley Gardens

This view of the Grand Hotel and Valley Gardens is a real puzzle, as it is taken from a postcard which bears a franking dated 18 November 1904, yet until 1911, the Valley Gardens at bottom was divided from the upper portion of the photograph, known as Collins' Field, by a stout stone wall. In this view, which must date from *c*.1903-04, there is not a trace of the wall, clearly visible in photographs of the same period. Further, the land at upper right has been planted, and yet such planting did not occur until 1911 at the earliest. Yet the card is clearly marked 1904! The Grand Hotel had been opened on 23 May 1903, having been designed by the Hartlepool architect, Christopher Brown, and built by Harrogate's own David Simpson.

It was in an ideal position, overlooking the popular Valley Gardens, and within easy reach of the local hunting and shooting amenities, which were once such an important aspect of life at the Spa. The seats, still a feature on the streets and in the parks of Harrogate, show the traditional 'serpent' design, so typical of health centres, being fitted with wooden backs and bases by the Harrogate carpenter, Alan Smith, whose workshop had been established in the old Paris Pavilion, just off Cold Bath Road. In this photograph, the footpath at centre top, decorated with two floral hoops now leads to the entrance to the sun colonnade.

Advertiser reader Mr C. Hopes advises that some of these early cards were subject to editing. [Supplied by Mr S. Townson]

Harrogate postcards forgeries or editings?

The previous picture shows a postcard view of the Valley Gardens and Grand Hotel which carried a franking of 1904 yet which showed a view of the gardens which could not have existed before 1911. The two postcard views shown on this page confirm that the practice of editing or 'touching up', did indeed occur. The first shows a view of the Royal Bath Winter Gardens, taken before World War One. The second is the identical photograph after it has been 'improved'.

At far left, the plebeian figure of the gardener, with his cloth cap and hoe, has been replaced by an elegantly dressed gentleman in top hat, accompanied by a lady. Below the corner of the building, the first picture shows a nanny with her infant charge, but in the edited version, a smart couple appear – he with straw boater and cane, she with bonnet and parasol. At dead centre, just behind the rockery, the same gentleman in straw boater may be seen in both pictures, but the equally elegant couple walking away from the camera in the upper view have been reversed, so that they appear to be walking towards it. The sharp-eyed will spot other editings. [Both cards and information supplied by Mr Clifford Hopes]

Progress with new Swimming Pool

If the crumbling lavatories at Pierhead were a reproof to the Harrogate of the 1990s, then the magnificent new Hydro Swimming Pool, opened in 1999, was a credit. Central Harrogate's first public swimming pool was built on the Dragon Estate at the corner of Dragon and Skipton Roads. Designed by the local firm of Bown, it was soundly built, and served the town well, until it began to show signs of wear in the early 1960s. Rather than repair the building, the Council decided to construct a new pool on a fresh site, and to sell the old one for housing. Accordingly, the *Advertiser* reported on 19 September 1964, that a contract to build a new pool on a site at Coppice Beck, had been awarded to Harrogate contractors Messrs W. G. Birch and Co Ltd. Loan sanction was sought for the sum of £242,834, the new pool measuring 82 feet, 6 inches long, and 42 feet in width, compared to the old pool's measurements of 75 feet by 30 feet. The provision of a learner's pool was a welcome innovation, and the spectators' gallery provided accommodation for 312 people.

Work began in January 1965, and the chairman of Harrogate's Wells and Baths committee and [*Advertiser* readers may need to be reminded that at this time, Harrogate was still a working Spa] Councillor Eric Oddy, gave an enthusiastic interview to the press, stating that the Borough Engineer's Department and the Quantity Surveyor, should be congratulated on the accuracy and fullness of the details they had prepared for tendering firms. This photograph was taken on 18 March 1966, and shows the interior of the new pool with its south-facing wall, the opening of which had been fixed for July 1966. In September, however, the *Advertiser* reported that everything was still not ship-shape, and this seems to have stimulated the public to make a number of criticisms about the new baths. Stung by this, Councillor Oddy reminded the Council that there was no comparison between the old baths and the new. He was right enough. The old baths had served Harrogate well for nearly 65 years, the new ones would last for little over 30. This was little short of scandalous. All of Harrogate must hope that the Hydro of 1999 lasts longer than the wretched thing it replaced.

A Grand Harrogate Outing, c.1910

One sign of the importance of the coach outing in the suggested itinerary of visitors to Harrogate, was the list of recommended places of interest published in the various guides to Harrogate. The *New Harrogate Guide* of 1812 recommends visits to 'Almas Cliff, Aldburgh, Boroughbridge, Brimham Rocks, Bolton Abbey, Cowthorpe, Fountains Abbey, Harewood, Hackfall, Knaresborough, Newby, Plumpton, Studley Spofford &c'. Such outings had long been the norm for visitors to Harrogate. In 1706, Nicholas Blundell described visits by coach to both 'Knesbrough and Stockhild', in the course of a visit to Harrogate to drink the waters. Similarly, in 1756, the widow of Bishop Hare describes some of the guests at the Queen Hotel hiring a special waggon to take them to Studley and Ripon. Accompanied by Lord Willoughby and some other gentlemen, the party 'trotted away very expeditiously to see Studley… danced till two in the morning, and came home as gaily as we went, highly pleased with the frolic'. In the late 19th and early 20th centuries, such outings were usually arranged either by the hotels, or private transportation businesses, many of which operated from St Mary's Walk and the Esplanade in Low Harrogate.

The photograph reproduced here is a great curiosity, as it shows a coach at Blubberhouses on the Harrogate, Skipton, Otley and Blubberhouses turnpike. The Frankland Arms Inn may be seen, which closed in 1903, and demolished in 1907, the stone being used to build the Meagill Lane Cemetery. The coach party, well wrapped up for the outing, is pulled by a team of four horses and has stopped at the Frankland Arms Inn for refreshments. An ostler has changed the horses, while at the very back of the coach may be seen the postilion's horn, which was always sounded as the coach rolled down Ripon Road into Harrogate. [Supplied by Mr & Mrs C. F. Holmes]

Lord Tennyson in Queen Parade

Despite its atrocious 20th-century intrusions, Queen Parade may still be considered one of Harrogate's finest streets. Because of its connection with the old Queen Hotel, having been laid out in the 1850s on land to the rear of that celebrated establishment, Queen Parade is certainly part of High Harrogate. Until World War Two, it presented a perfect example of mid and late Victorian residential planning, including terraces, semi-detached, and single mansion properties. Although the loss of the ornamental railings in the 1940 'salvage' drive damaged the traditional Victorian appearance of the parade, it was not until the 1960s that the western side suffered the first of a series of demolitions which saw the replacement of three significant buildings.

The first was 'Pembroke' House, a huge and gaunt looking pile which had the air of the infamous Borley Rectory, supposedly the most haunted house in England. This was actually the home of High Harrogate College, after it moved from the old Dragon Hotel. The Headmaster, Walter Kaye, was a fine antiquary, and his book *Records of Harrogate*, is the most important book on early Harrogate that has yet been written. Oak Lodge, at the northwest corner of Victoria Avenue, was a large villa, which for a time housed a Christian association for youth. Between the demolished Oak Lodge, and the handsome pair of houses at the junction with North Park Road, known

as Grove Villas, there once stood Clifton House, which after being a lodging house, became home to Clifton College Boys' School.

Back in 1863, this was where Alfred, Lord Tennyson, stayed during his visit to Harrogate, and his wife wrote a letter from Clifton House, Queen Parade, on 14 August. Tennyson did not enjoy his visit, as the weather was cold and wet, although he stayed until 10 September, drinking the Sulphur Water and taking a few excursions.

After being demolished in the 1970s, the name of Clifton House was retained for Clifton House Flats. At one time, every residence in Queen Parade had a name, but recent stone cleaning seems to have removed several examples from house façades. For example, on the east side, beginning at North Park Road, there was Wentworth House, followed by the terrace of Eaton House, Hall Garth Lodge, and Beulah Lodge. Then came the detached Wetherby House, overlooking Victoria Avenue, and the pair of villas fronted with superb glazed iron verandas, Maryville and Hedley House. Further on, towards York Place, came Burley Lodge, Chatham Lodge – now divided between Stone Close and Seventeen – and finally, Melbourne Lodge. If names of famous English politicians were considered appropriate for Victoria Avenue, it should possess a Disraeli Villa and a Palmerston Lodge!

Lord Baden Powell on the Stray

The previous article referred to Clifton House School, in Queen Parade, and the story is now taken up after it removed to a site overlooking Tewit Well. This unique photograph shows the founder of the Boy Scout movement, Lord Robert Baden Powell, on south Stray on 9 July 1921. Lord Baden Powell was in Harrogate for the special purpose of presenting Peter's Pole to the Clifton House School Pack, which had won the award of best pack in the United Kingdom, an exceptional commendation.

The *Advertiser* reported that: 'After the salute, the 10th Harrogate pack gave the grand howl, and the Chief Scout then presented Peter's Pole to the 10th Harrogate – Clifton House – Wolf Cub pack. Sixer Roper receiving it on behalf of his colleagues. The pole is named after Baden Powell's son, Peter, and is presented to the pack which gains the most marks for efficiency. Commander Dr Laura Veale was also present.'

This photograph does not show the somewhat tattered Union flag which was flying over south Stray on this occasion. The flag had been the one which had flown over Fort Ayre, at Mafeking, and after the Relief of Mafeking in May 1900, this flag had been acquired by a Scoutmaster of the 1st Harrogate Troop. On 9 May 1999, the 10th Harrogate (St Wilfrid's) Walsh's Own Scout Group celebrated 21 years of Scouting at St Wilfrid's, and 90 years of Scouting since the 10th Harrogate was formed at Clifton House School. [Supplied by Mr R. Langley]

Royal Baths Grand Pump Room

The Grand Pump Room of the Royal Baths, as photographed *c.*1962, when it was still used to dispense the Mineral Waters. At this time, the waters were pumped to the great octagonal mahogany counter, which within a few years was to be chopped up by order of the Corporation, as a 'redundant' feature. Also visible is the wonderful terrazzo floor, carpeted over in about 1970, but which survives, awaiting restoration in a more appreciative age. One element in the decoration of the Grand Pump Room of the Royal Baths, which has survived many changes of taste, is the frieze which encircles the whole area, containing lines of verse. Some of these lines are well known, such as:

> Ah what avail the largest gifts of heaven,
> When drooping health and spirits go amiss,
> How tasteless then whatever can be given,
> Health is the vital principle of bliss,
> And exercise of health.

These lines come from James Thompson's epic poem *Castle of Indolence, c.*1748 but the authorship of the other verse has for many years been a complete mystery:

> Then in life's goblet freely press,
> The leaves that give it bitterness,
> Nor prize the healing waters less,
> For in thy darkness and distress,
> New light and strength they give.

But see the next article for details of their authorship!

A Poet's Lodging

The verses engraved on the frieze of the Grand Pump Room of the Royal Baths include: 'Then in life's goblet freely press, The leaves that give it bitterness,' which are from the poem *Youth Renewed*, written by Montgomery [1771-1854]. This was not the same Montgomery whose poems were highly praised by the popular press, before being mercilessly ridiculed by Lord Macauley, whose critique included the cutting observation that 'his writing bears the same relation to poetry which a Turkey carpet bears to a picture'.

The Harrogate verses were by his brother, James, a fine Scottish poet, who visited Harrogate in 1821, 1825, 1826 and 1846, staying at the Cornwall House lodgings run by Mrs Benson. James Montgomery visited Harrogate to recover his health, and it was during his 1825 visit that he wrote the poem *Youth Renewed*. The fourth edition of the *Oxford Companion to English Literature* rather unfairly excludes James Montgomery, so it is interesting to recall that when our Victorian predecessors decided to embellish the Royal Baths with verse, they selected lines written in Harrogate back in 1825. The accompanying photograph shows Cornwall House – the big bow-windowed Georgian house – some 75 years after Montgomery's 1825 visit, and about 30 years before the houses at extreme left were demolished to improve the entrance to Valley Gardens.

Crowds on Montpellier Stray, *c.*1910, watching Professor Candler's Punch and Judy show.

E. D. Briggs & Co, outfitters, were at the corner of Cheltenham Parade and King's Road from *c.*1904 to 1907.

The beautiful King's Road promenade, dedicated to the memory of Edward VII, seen *c.*1912.

West Park's Clarendon Hotel, victim to the 1970s demolition mania.

The Harrogate Pierrots returning homewards after an afternoon's performance.

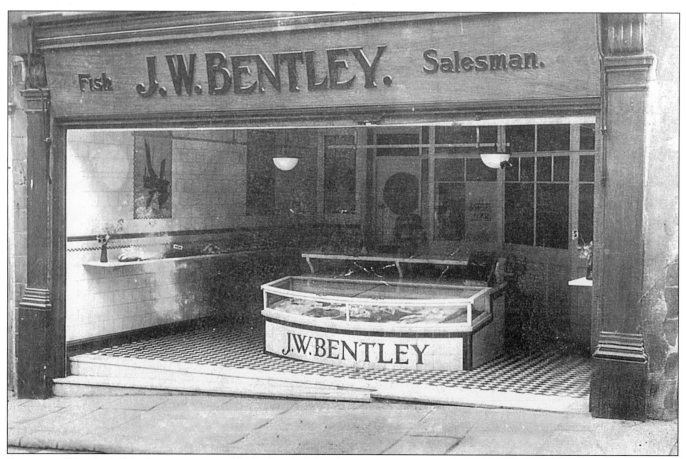

Frontage of Bentley's fish shop, at corner of Oxford and Union Street, *c.*1920.

The Central Cinema

Pedestrians viewing the site opposite the Harrogate Theatre, filled in 1998 by the architecturally impoverished Marks & Spencer store, may be interested to recall that this was once occupied by the Central Cinema, reached through a little arcade of shops. The Central Cinema had been built by Alderman Houfe, an architect, for the Central Cinema Ltd., and opened on 31 July 1920 with a seating capacity of 1,100. Sound recording had been demonstrated in Harrogate as early as July 1891, when an audience in the Spa Rooms was treated to a performance of Edison's Phonograph. Moving Pictures had been seen in Harrogate in April 1907 with a display of 'animated picture displays' which thrilled audiences at the St James's Hall.

However, the *Harrogate Advertiser* for 25 May 1929 reported that '*The Singing Fool*, the first full-length talkie to be shown in Harrogate, has had a tremendous success this week. The Central Cinema is filled to capacity nightly...' What the *Advertiser* had of course forgotten was that talking pictures had already been shown in Harrogate at the Royal Hall in 1921, using a system of sound and image synchronisation invented by the town's own Claude Verity! The Central Cinema was demolished in 1961 but the former St James's Hall, Lowther Arcade, and a rare surviving terrace of Georgian stone cottages were razed only in 1998 to clear the way for the present mediocrity.

St Mary's Church

The present church of St Mary's, opened in 1916, is actually a replacement for the earlier church of St Mary which had been closed in 1904 after being declared unsafe. The first St Mary's Church had been built in 1824-25 in order to provide Low Harrogate with an appropriate counterpart to High Harrogate's Chapel of St John. A petition to the Duchy of Lancaster in 1821 had received a favourable response, and following the collection of various subscriptions, the architect of the Royal Bath Hospital, Samuel Chapman, was commissioned to design the new building. At a cost of £3,137, the new church was the most expensive ecclesiastical building ever put up in Harrogate at that time.

This print depicts old St Mary's more or less from the garden of the present Beech Lodge on the Esplanade. An idea of the appearance of old St Mary's may be had from an examination subject to the owners permission of the Chapel of Harrogate Ladies College, which was built from material assembled from the church when it was dismantled after 1904. Although Harrogate people probably take for granted the availability of so many fine churches in their town, it is possible that, one day, they may become a tourist attraction.

Beulah Street

Beulah Street owes its existence to an old right of way which ran from York Place, via Albert Terrace, and down as far as the Wesleyan Methodist Chapel, built in 1824 at the corner of Beulah Street and the modern Oxford Street. At first, its buildings were primarily cottage dwellings – some of which still survive behind the modern frontages of the south-eastern section of Beulah Street next to its junction with Cambridge Street – with a few single-storey commercial premises. In this photograph of *c.*1880 may be seen the older single-storeyed premises together with their replacements still in the course of erection. It seems that the lower building was dismantled and moved further up Beulah Street, where it was extended and provided with a central arcade. This structure survives to this day, though in a somewhat altered form. Beulah Street was converted into a pleasant pedestrian zone in 1998.

Woodlands House

One of Harrogate's lesser known lost monuments, Woodlands House developed from an 18th century cottage property into a splendid residence which was advertised in the *York Herald* for 22 June 1822 in the following manner: Woodlands – to be let. A good dwelling house, situated on the south side of Dr Jaques's plantations, consisting of a drawing room, large dining room, store room, six good lodging rooms, kitchen, pantries, dairy, cellar, coach house, stables, good garden &c, with or without land. Woodlands was adjacent to Hookstone Road, near to the junction with Wetherby Road, and had once been owned by Lord Loughborough (Alexander Wedderburn), who in all probability resided here during the construction of Wedderburn House. This photograph dates from November 1965, shortly before the building was demolished to make way for the brick houses which replaced it.

Royal Bath Hospital

This photograph shows the Royal Bath Hospital shortly after the major rebuilding of 1889 which had been made possible thanks to generous charitable gifts from people such as Queen Victoria and Samson Fox. The handsome Scottish baronial style of architecture had been made popular by the late Prince Consort, especially at Balmoral, and the whole ensemble had been designed to harmonise with the surrounding Valley Gardens, in which patients and their visitors were encouraged to exercise. The institution of the Royal Bath Hospital owed its existence to charitable subscription, in that the land had been given by the Earl of Harewood, and the cost of building by subscriptions from visitors to the inns. When the hospital first opened in 1824-25, it was as a direct result of a charitable munificence which continued unabated into the 20th century.

The appalling act of closure in 1994 and the subsequent removal of facilities to Leeds, severed a connection with the Valley Gardens of 170 years of historic service. The belated announcement by the British Prime Minister as to the importance of small hospitals to local communities, came too late to reverse Harrogate's loss. The buildings which in 1994 were threatened with total demolition by applicant developer Bryant Homes, were saved by another company, Crosby Homes, whose 'Sovereign Court' is a model example of how to convert historic premises into successful residential use.

Cambridge Crescent

This attractive photograph of Cambridge Crescent must have been taken soon after the unveiling of the town's War Memorial on 2 June 1922. At centre may be seen the premises of Betty's Café, then at their original location. To their right, and just beneath the tower of St Luke's Church, stand the works and shop of Phillipson's Pianos, which occupied the building which had once been the manse for Wesley Chapel. The perpendicular gothic window belonged to St Peter's School, which was located at this site from its establishment in 1865 until 1936, when it was demolished to make way for the Regal Cinema. At extreme right may be seen St Peter's Church itself, still without its great square tower, which was not to be completed until 1926. Perhaps the most interesting aspect of this photograph is that it contains a unique view of the last surviving original frontage to Cambridge Crescent, then occupied by Lloyd's Bank. This shows a superbly proportioned façade, and it is a thousand pities that not one of the original frontages designed by Hirst and built by George Dawson from 1867-68, has survived.

Belle Vue

To obtain an idea of the location of Belle Vue House, it is necessary to walk along Oxford Street until the premises of British Home Stores are reached, and, standing before their window, project your gaze about 20 yards into the shop. This was where Belle Vue House once stood. Built in 1826 by captain Thomas Thrush, RN, Belle Vue was once one of the two principal residences of Oxford Street (known as Chapel Street before 1908), the other being Prospect Cottage. Captain Thrush became a national celebrity in 1825, when he resigned his highly-prized Royal Navy Commission on the grounds that it was impossible to be a Christian and a Military Officer. Rejected by his former colleagues and ostracised by society, Captain Thrush retreated into Belle Vue House from where he issued a series of polemical pamphlets. The house took its name from the view across an unbuilt Cheltenham estate, with green fields which stretched as far as the crown of Ripon Road. Behind the property, a garden stretched back to the footpath which later became Cambridge Street. Belle Vue was demolished in 1969 when Marks & Spencer extended their premises back into Oxford Street.

High Harrogate

When this drawing of High Harrogate was made in 1829, plans were under way to replace the old Chapel of St John, at far right, with a more commodious structure, completed by 1831. Although the new Christ Church was a great improvement, the materials from the old Chapel did not go to waste, but were re-erected in James Street as the Victoria Hall, on the site later occupied by Beattie's Toy Shop. At centre, the drawing shows Church Square with a gap where the Church School would some eight years later be erected. The lordly Granby at far left, was still the most prestigious address in Harrogate, and when it was sold in 1824 at an auction opposite the Bank of England in London, it was described as 'one of the first Inns in the United Kingdom'. The same roads and footpaths still cross the Stray today, but the cows went long ago.

Somerset Lodgings

This undated photograph taken from the top of Parliament Street must have been shortly before the old Somerset Hotel, seen at far right with its columned portico, was rebuilt in 1869. The two-storeyed regency-fronted building to the immediate left of the old Somerset is Somerset House, also known as Somerset Lodgings. This seems to be the oldest surviving structure in Parliament Street, dating from the 1790s, being designed with beautiful bow windows so typical of the best Georgian architecture.

Somerset House had been the home of the builder John Thompson, whose work included the Victoria Hotel, the old Somerset Hotel, and the Harlow Hill Observation Tower. It is an odd world when breweries spend a fortune importing fake antiques to give pubs an atmosphere of age, while at the same time they destroy centuries of history by changing pub names to conform with some ephemeral and vulgar fashion.

Thus Harrogate has within a few years lost its Alexandra, its Devonshire, its Grand, its Muckles, its Prospect, its Ship, and its Somerset – some of them names which reached back for centuries. What comes next? Will there be a craze for Spanish theme pubs, or Greek theme pubs? Can we expect Hale's Bar to become Zorba's Bar, or the Coach and Horses to adopt the name of Red Hanrahan's poteen? But at least the old High Harrogate Devonshire has regained its historic title, after having suffered the indignity of being named 'Molly Malone's' for a couple of years. Somerset House was thoroughly refurbished in 1999.

Spa Rooms Terrace

This photograph of *c*.1871 is topical for two reasons. The view is that of the pleasure gardens behind the Spa Rooms, which were remodelled in 1871 to provide an improved range of amenities for visitors a skating rink, a bandstand, statuary, footpaths through replanted grounds, and fountains carved by James Simpson. The steps at far left enabled visitors to descend from the back of the Spa Rooms and into the beautifully maintained gardens which stretched back to the site of the modern Conference Centre. These steps still survive, although they are totally hidden by the exhibition halls which have grown round the site since 1959.

But what, it may be asked, has happened to the lions? When the Spa Rooms were dismantled in 1939, much of the statuary from the gardens was sold, the lions being purchased by the late Alderman Spenceley, who re-erected them outside his property in Station Parade which in more recent times became Carrington's night club. However, the lions have since been removed. Another pair of lions, which flanked the Ripon Road entrance, may still be seen at Harlow Car gardens, guarding the approaches to the re-erected Spa Rooms colonnade.

Parliament Street Footpath

It is fascinating to compare the alignment and width of the main footpath which runs along the eastern edge of Ripon Road and Parliament Street, over an interval of over 130 years. By the mid-1860s, the eastern half of Parliament Street was filled with shops and lodging houses, and had a pavement some 15 feet in width. As can be seen, the footpath was in exact alignment with the Ripon Road footpath, which passed the boundary railings of the Spa Rooms estate. At right, the site of the Royal Baths was filled with trees belonging to the Montpellier Baths, whilst across Crescent Road, a strip of the Stray may be seen, which at this time had not been fashioned into Crescent Gardens But just take a look at things today. The Parliament Street footpath has been cut to a fraction of its once generous width, and the Ripon Road footpath has been savagely attacked and all for the convenience of the car user. But is there really any need to always make such changes at the expense of the pedestrian?

Cambridge Street, c.1962

Out of a total of nine buildings shown in this photograph of *c.*1962, only two now remain. From left to right may be seen: (1) the entrance to the Ebor pub, demolished in 1907 to make way for the vile concrete box containing Burton's; (2) the single-storey structure containing Halford's Cards; (3) Lowther Arcade; (4) the historic St James's Hall, then occupied by Thrift Stores; (5) the former Conservative Club at the corner of Cambridge and Beulah Streets; (6) the Harrogate Bus Station, above which may be seen (7) the backs of the houses built by Richard Ellis in East Parade; (8) Goodrick's Chambers, and (9) the second Harrogate Market Building of 1933-39.

Of the seven demolished buildings, our greatest regret should be for the Bus Station, which was placed wonderfully well to serve the public, responsibility for the loss of which must be placed with the late Nicholas Ridley MP. Lowther Arcade, which should have been restored after the fire of 1988, was instead flattened along with the delightful old Ship Inn, by GRE Properties, who announced a plan to rebuild the entire site with 'much-needed medium-size retail units'. These units were so much needed that after the site had been flatted, GRE abandoned their scheme. And then along came dear old Marks & Spencer, who generously bought the site and erected a new store in the neo-banal style of architecture. At the time of writing, only two of the buildings in this photograph remain.

The Mercer Art Gallery

The continual series of superb exhibitions displayed at the Mercer Art Gallery serve to remind people that – apart from a brief period as offices for the town's administration – the building has always served as a centre for entertainment and instruction. Built in 1805-06 by a group of local doctors as an amenity for visitors to the Low Harrogate Spa, the Promenade Rooms were a centre for fashionable assembly. Visitors could not only promenade, gossip and ogle the famous, but playing cards, newspapers, books, and musical recitals were also provided. Entertainers were

employed, such as jugglers, singers and comics, and, eventually, literary lectures became a regular feature.

Henry Morton Stanley thrilled his audience with an account of his meeting with Dr Livingstone, Lily Langtree performed *School for Scandal*, and Oscar Wilde described his recent tour of the USA. It was during the 1880s that Harrogate Amateur Minstrels set up the Old Town Hall Theatre, thanks in no small part to the efforts of W. H. Breare. In this photograph of *c.*1890, the gate posts and ornamental railings, enclosing the garden, may be seen.

Station Square

An uncommon view of Station Square, taken from the grounds of the Railway Station in about 1905. At this time, the station was provided with an attractive 'fringe' of gardens and ornamental iron railings, which contributed to the appearance of Station Square. The late Alderman Richard Ellis had been particularly keen to smarten up this part of town, as it was the very first impression of Harrogate to be had by visitors arriving by rail. Ellis himself had built the magnificent terrace in James' Street which runs from the Yorkshire Bank as far as the Station Hotel, the latter being erected in two parts: the section shown in this card having been put up in 1873 to a design by Arthur Hiscoe, who was also the architect of the old Market, as well as of the 1874 remodelling of the Mercer Art Gallery.

The second section of the Station Hotel was built in 1890 by Bown, who followed Hiscoe's design with admirable care, and which carried it round into Albert Street. A short time after this postcard was issued, the Station Hotel was provided with two elaborate entrance canopies of decorative iron and stained glass, both of which were needlessly demolished after World War Two. To the right of the picture, the Jubilee Statue, given to the town in 1887 by Richard Ellis in honour of Queen Victoria's Golden Jubilee. The Queen turns her back on the ramshackle buildings on the north of the square, gazing across to the site of the unbuilt town hall. [Supplied by S. Townson]

The junction of Parliament Street and King's Road, *c.*1923.

When this photograph was taken in about 1907, Church Square's 'Stray View' still possessed its splendid railings and ionic porticos.

Kursaal Grounds

Here is a good view of the eastern façade of the Kursaal, taken shortly after its completion in 1903. The photograph appears to have been taken from the site of the former boating lake, which had grown from the streams which poured down into Low Harrogate from the Cold Bath Road and St Mary's area. After flowing through a culvert in Crescent Gardens, the streams crossed Ripon Road beneath a little bridge, before mingling with the waters from what later became known as the Springfield Estate. Along with surface drainage water, the springs included a considerable amount of raw sewage, which eventually formed a lake in the gardens of the Spa Rooms.

The offensive smells arising from this lake caused much annoyance, and throughout the 1860s and early 1870s the Towns Improvement Commissioners, and the Public Rooms company which ran the Spa Rooms, were often obliged to deal with complaints from the public. The matter was resolved to the satisfaction of all the parties through the construction of further culverts to link the drainage to the Coppice Beck, and by replacing the lake with a skating rink in 1875. The skating rink was finally removed in about 1900 when the area was cleared for the erection of the Kursaal. One very important aspect of the new Kursaal's facilities was to enable visitors to enjoy the beautiful gardens which had grown on the Spa Rooms estate since 1835.

This postcard view shows, at far right, the steps which led from the Kursaal's rear promenade down on to the rolling lawns, upon which Edwardian visitors delighted to stroll after evening concerts. At far left may be seen the eastern façade of the Spa Rooms, beyond which lay King's Road. It is pleasant to know that most of this splendid promenade of decorative iron and stained glass has survived, and the Harrogate International Centre intend to restore the feature as an important element of the newly refurbished Royal Hall, as the Kursaal is now known. [Supplied by Mr S. Townson]

Old Queen's Head Inn

It would be surprising if many readers are familiar with this limited edition postcard, which reproduces a view of the old Queen's Head Inn which was reported as being a youthful effort of the great artist William Powell Frith, *c*.1833. Frith's father took over the Dragon Hotel, which along with the Queen and Granby, was one of the great hostelries of High Harrogate. The young Frith is supposed to have sketched much of Harrogate before he left for London in 1835, including all three of High Harrogate's big hotels.

The drawing shows the Queen's Head Inn from York Place, before the major rebuilding of the 1850s. At far right may be seen the ballroom, with its tall ground floor windows, still visible today. The central portico and balancing wing have yet to be added to the older portion shown here. It was at the Queen's Head Inn that a celebrated event occurred in 1767, with the arrival of a commercial traveller, or 'rider' called Joseph Booth. This Booth was employed by a Mr Cookson of Newcastle-upon-Tyne, and he broke his journey overnight at Harrogate, riding into town from the Knaresborough Road. Like many underlings freed from the firm control of their employer, Joseph Booth was determined to enjoy himself at someone else's expense, and his arrival at the fashionable resort of Harrogate in the company of his masters money gave him the opportunity to indulge himself.

Passing the lordly Granby, who would never have allowed a mere commercial traveller to pass its doors, Joseph came to the Queen's Head, and decided to spend a night there. To impress everyone, he throws his weight around, and orders an impossibly huge dinner of two fat ducks and a peck of peas. The farce begins when his master and mistress arrive at the Inn, to be told that the last dinner ducks have been ordered by an important guest! This story was written up as a poem in 1771, which in turn formed the inspiration for a play of 1777 called *Ducks and Pease*, or, the *Newcastle Rider* by John Lund. The play was last published in 1838 by Pickersgill Palliser of Harrogate, founder of this newspaper. The author was therefore delighted to receive a new edition of this play and poem, published in December 1996 by Bill Taylor of Harrogate, in a beautiful, limited edition, being one of several fine editions he has produced over the years.

The Old Swan's Hornblower

Aircraft Production and the Ministry of Supply, being derequisitioned only in 1948. When the hotel was re-opened officially on 1 July 1948, it was in a somewhat shabby condition. Thanks, however, to the general manager, Mr G. A. Wright, it began a programme of improvements, including the then unusual feature of a day nursery, and re-adoption of the Swan name this time to be known as the Old Swan. An establishment such as the Swan would have had a Hornblower in the 18th century, to announce the arrival and departure of coaches, when the post lapsed – at a guess, though it is not known – was probably after the arrival of the railways in Harrogate ensured the end of the stage-coach era.

Certainly, it was Mr Wright who re-introduced the Hornblower in 1953, by his invitation to Mr Bill Harding, pictured in this photograph, to announce the arrival of motor coaches, as well as sounding a 'time please gentlemen' call for the bar. Another of Mr Wright's improvements was the restoration of the Tudor-style bar, with its reminders

From its humble origins as an 18th-century inn, the Swan grew to be an important hotel in the 19th century, under the ownership of the Shutt family. A major reconstruction occurred in 1878, when the Swan became the Harrogate Hydro, and a dry house into the bargain. During World War Two, the Harrogate Hydro was occupied by the Ministry of of the coaching era wooden floors, oak-beamed ceilings, pewter pots and gleaming horns, all typical of the days when coaches such as the *True Blue*, the *Tally-Ho* and the *Rocket* would roll into Harrogate to disgorge another set of visitors, whose arrival would be heralded by the Hornblower's call. [Supplied by Mrs Mary Brown]

Winter Garden

The Winter Garden was built as an integral part of the Royal Baths, whose 100th anniversary was celebrated in 1997. Doctors had, for centuries, recognised the medical advantages of exercise in conjunction with the Harrogate 'cure' of drinking the mineral waters and living a relaxed, stress-free life. The laying out of the Stray in the 1770s was an early example of this recognition. In the 19th century, the Victorians understood that for the infirm, exercise out of doors was not always desirable, and that walks protected from the weather were a necessary amenity for a modern spa.

Accordingly, spas were provided with glazed promenades, those in Harrogate first being built on the Spa Rooms estate next to the modern Royal Hall. It was therefore natural that when the winners of the Royal Baths' competition, Baggalley & Bristow, completed their plans, a Winter Garden was included. When the Winter Garden was demolished in 1938, the splendid 'Merry Widow' staircase which formed the Parliament Street entrance, survived, as it does to this day, together with a section of the glass roof. [Supplied by Mr S. Townson]

The Market Clock

More letters must be received by the *Harrogate Advertiser* on the subject of the fate of the old Market Clock than about any other subject of local history. This photograph shows the soot-blackened clock tower of the market shortly after the disastrous fire of 31 January 1937. At left may be seen the Cambridge Street façade of the market, over which range the new Woolworth's building, the fine Victorian tower of the Lowther Arcade and the St James's Hall. Right of the Clock Tower is Benefit Footware, at the corner of Beulah Street, and at far right, the premises of Howden's Garage, demolished *c.*1953 for the Station Square improvements.

The Clock Tower, built in 1876-77 to a splendid neo-renaissance design of Harrogate architect Hiscoe, received its clock in May 1877. This clock, built by the world-famous firm of Potts of Leeds, was a gift to Harrogate from the Baroness Angela Burdett-Coutts (a great philanthropist, and friend of Charles Dickens), who had developed a great affection for Harrogate. It survived a serious fire in 1914, and also the fire of 1937, after which it was dismantled prior to being re-erected in the new market built by Leonard

Clark the following year. When plans were announced to replace Clark's building with the new Victoria Centre in the late 1980s, there was common feeling in Harrogate that the Baroness's clock must be saved, and consequently, when demolition began, it was dismantled and the mechanism put into the safe keeping of the Harrogate Museum. There was also an agreement on the part of Speyhawk, the developer, that the clock would be installed in an appropriate clock tower on some neighbouring location.

However, as is well known Speyhawk began their redevelopment at the beginning of the recession, and encountered severe financial difficulties, which resulted in the unfinished Victoria Centre being taken over by National Provident. It seems that National Provident took on Speyhawk's obligations – among which was the undertaking to reinstate the clock. Now although it would have been unreasonable to press National Provident to provide a clock tower at the height of the recession, with the Victoria Centre barely occupied, things are somewhat different today. Surely to goodness something can be done about the clock tower!

Opening of the Royal Baths Western Wing

At the time of writing, there has been a lot of debate on the future of the Royal Baths, building and the fate of its redundant 'western wing'. It is therefore particularly appropriate to publish this photograph of part of the ceremony which accompanied the opening of the same building in 1939. It has been kindly lent by Mrs Lunn of Harrogate, whose husband stands to the far right of the Guard of Honour. The old building of the Royal Baths had been opened by HRH the Duke of Cambridge in 1897, during the high summer of Queen Victoria's Diamond Jubilee. Only a few years later, it became clear to the authorities that further facilities were necessary to accommodate the increasing numbers of visitors to the Spa, and in 1929 the borough engineer drew up extensive plans to extend the Royal Baths southwards as far as the Ginnell, and to draw out the porte-cochère into Crescent Gardens.

These plans remained unfulfilled, but in the 1930s,

following their abandonment of the last two phases of the Sun Pavilion project, the Council switched to a new scheme for enlarging the Royal Baths. A large block for treatments was provided, along with a great hall for public meetings and concerts, and a Fountain Court. The construction was made possible only after the demolition of the Victorian Winter Garden, which had been an integral part of the original Royal Baths. The new buildings were opened in great style on 10 July 1939, by the Lord Mayor of London, Sir Frank Bowater, and received much praise, not only for their elaborate treatment facilities, but for the impressive Lounge Hall, with its superb panelling and richly-coffered ceiling, which soon became central to the performing arts in Harrogate. In this photograph, men of the Territorial Army Prince of Wales' 5th West Yorkshire Regiment – 'B' Company, provide a Guard of Honour for the Lord Mayor. [Supplied by Mrs Lunn]

The old Wellington Inn

An *Advertiser* reader has supplied some extracts from a journal written in the 1840s by his great-great-grandfather.

18 September 1844:

'From Leeds we proceeded to Harewood Bridge, stop'd to Bait (the horses) and get dinner. It was a very pretty Inn situate at the end of the Bridge crossing the Wharfe… There appear to be fishing rods kept at the House for the use of visitors to fish in the river. They charged us 1s 9d each for a mutton chop dinner. We now proceeded on to Harrogate, we kept on apparently higher ground than I expected, we arrived at Harrogate about dusk, drove to the Wellington, they were full, we sought out private lodgings and met with very good and comfortable sitting room… 16 feet 7 inches by about 15 feet; 3 beds and the room £2 5s 0d per week. Boarded ourselves at Mrs Linforth's, 1 Grove Terrace next but one above the Wellington. Our Mrs included cooking in at this. I liked it much better

myself than being at a Public House, because we could get our meals when we liked and what we liked, we were all for plain living. No drinking. 19th Friday. This morning we all went to drink the sulphur water and paid 1s each as subscription a week for it and the room. I took very little, David and Thomas took more freely. Mine operated but I believe I should have been better without it.' On the penultimate day of the visit to Harrogate, the group 'spent a little time pleasantly in the Promenade grounds, I after thought that I had not become a subscriber for the week as it is only 4s/6d and one gets to see daily papers &c.'

This last reference is to the building which now houses the Mercer Art Gallery in Swan Road, which had been originally built as an Assembly Room and Promenade in 1806. No picture of the Promenade in 1844 seems to have survived, but the accompanying photograph shows the Wellington Inn, in Cold Bath Road, as it would have appeared to the visitors of that time.

The Grand Opera House

Here is a fine view of Harrogate's Grand Opera House as it looked shortly after being opened on 13 January 1900. The Opera House – which was in reality built for the performance of plays – featured *The Gentlemen in Khaki* on its opening night, which was a charity performance dedicated to the victims of the South African War. The building had been designed by Frank Tugwell, who provided a rich plasterwork interior, and a quite outstanding Art Nouveau frieze in the entrance hall. A suspended canopy provided all-weather protection for pedestrians along the curtilage of the building. This canopy was demolished after World War Two, a most regrettable loss of a piece of street furniture which was not only useful, but attractive. Another lost amenity, depicted in this postcard, is the row of trees at far right which once lined Cheltenham Parade, and it would be sensible if these too could be replaced, in order to complement the work done by the private sector in improving so many of the properties between the Theatre and King's Road.

Avenue Hotel

Demolition, in 1972, of the former Avenue Hotel on the corner of Station Parade and Victoria Avenue deprived Central Harrogate of a fine and substantial Victorian building of *c.*1880, built as terrace housing, with three principal storeys, and an attic. The architect's name is currently unknown but one of the Bown brothers is a possibility as they often used the feature of double-arched upper windows in their designs. According to the *Yorkshire Post* of 27 May 1950, the houses were converted into an hotel 'some 25 years ago', and it was about to be 'taken over' by the government for use as offices. During the demolition, the contractors told the author that the building had been built superbly, and was very strongly put together. Its replacement, with an uncouth box of prefabricated units, is not an ornament to the town. The Avenue Hotel was flattened shortly after the demolition of the Lancaster Hotel, in Cold Bath Road, and shortly before the loss of the Clarendon Hotel on West Park, three buildings which contributed in a positive way to the attractiveness of the town, and whose loss represents an impoverishment of Harrogate's historic fabric.

Fred, in the author's opinion, is the best barber in Harrogate. He has cut his hair for the past 30 years, and when Fred talks about Harrogate, the author always listens. Accordingly, when Fred said: "What about all these toilets they're closing down? Why don't you write something about that?" the author knew he must rise to the challenge. So here goes! – but what to choose for a photograph? Then this photograph came to mind. It shows the controversial Prince of Wales lavatories being demolished in 1923. In the background rises the bulk of the Prince of Wales Hotel, with at right, the footpath leading to Trinity Church. In the past, Harrogate considered the provision of public lavatories to be an essential amenity for a town which specialised in providing visitors with medicinal waters, many of which were diuretic in effect.

The town also contained a high number of public houses and other places of refreshment, so it was obviously sensible to ensure that lavatories were available for anyone who required them, and up to World War One, there was no shortage of this amenity. However, the situation today has deteriorated to a level which would have been unimaginable to the authorities of the pre-1914 era. On taking an old ordnance map, and proceeding round the town centre in a clockwise direction, it may be noted that the following amenities had been closed

and demolished since World War One: (1) Next to the Royal Hall, junction of Rings Road and Ripon Road; (2) Royal Hall Gardens, end of King's Road; (3) Ship Yard, behind Woolworth's; (4) One Arch; (5) The Bus Station; (6) High Harrogate Stray at Walker's Passage; (7) Prince of Wales corner; (8) Junction of Otley Road and Harlow Moor Road; (9) back Valley Drive; (10) Pier Head. As the map does not go as far as New Park or Bilton, these areas are excluded, but ten closures is really quite bad enough. Most of these closures have occurred in recent times, probably since 1960.

What on earth are we playing at? It seems irresponsible to encourage visitors to come to Harrogate, to visit cafés, restaurants, pubs and wine bars where they are tempted to indulge in a high liquid intake and then to deny people conveniences. This is why so many shopkeepers begin their day by finding that the entrances to their premises are in an unpleasant condition. This is why the police arrest people for causing 'nuisances' but what are people supposed to do when all the conveniences are being closed down? It seems crazy. In the day time, visitors to the town centre make a bee-line for Betty's, but why should Betty's provide a public amenity which up to a few years ago existed in the neighbouring Pier Head lavatories? Enough – the point is made, and if some readers do not care for the subject, they can blame it on Fred.

Victoria Park Methodist Church

The Victoria Park Methodist Church is seen here in this photograph of *c.*1950, taken from the pavement in front of Handford & Dawson's chemist's shop. Richard Ellis – one of the greatest figures in the history of Harrogate – was a devoted Methodist, and a founder of the original Salem Chapel in James Street, referred to in an accompanying article about the Whitby Jet Manufacturer, Isaac Greebury.

The very first entry in the church accounts is a donation of £2 from Richard Ellis, and eventually, sufficient money was raised to enable the building of the James Street Chapel – today, Richard Shops. Eventually, the Salem Chapel became too small to accommodate the growing congregation, and a new site was required. Ellis, in the meantime, had been responsible for the formation of the Victoria Park Company, which planned to link High and Low Harrogate by the means of a number of splendid thoroughfares, including Victoria Avenue and Station Parade.

Ellis donated part of the land for the building of a new Methodist Church, and work began in September 1863. The church was designed by George Dawson's architect, J. H. Hirst of Bristol, the foundation stone being laid on 17 August 1864. Built in an unusual Victorian gothic style, at an estimated cost of £3,400, the church was opened for divine worship on 17 August 1865. The final cost has in the meantime risen to £4,955 9s 10d, the debt being cleared on both the church and its neighbouring Sunday School in 1885 by Richard Ellis.

In a further act of generosity, Ellis presented Richmond Villa in Raglan Street to the church as a manse for the minister, which function it served until being demolished in the following century to make way for the Court House. Sadly, the church which had been one of the loves of Richard Ellis's life, was demolished in spring 1954 with its site being converted into a temporary garden, before the building of the Co-op, now known as Sunwin House. It was reported that the organ was bought for use by the Meanwood Road Methodist Church in Leeds.

The Gardens of the Royal Baths and Winter Gardens

Writing of the Royal Baths and Winter Gardens, the *Harrogate Herald* of 14 April 1897 noted that the ornamental rockery – seen at right – was being completed under the supervision of the Clerk of Works, and that all of the grounds and bath-chair ramps were about to be asphalted to ensure that visitors and patients would have as smooth a footing as possible.

The Winter Gardens at left were to be fitted with electric lights, in time for the official opening in July 1897, and Alderman Fortune and the furniture sub-committee were authorised to visit Kirkstall Grange at Leeds, to view plants for the Winter Gardens. At right may be seen the entrance to the Peat Baths, erected 1909-11, at the recommendation of the personal physician to King Edward VII, Sir Frederic Treves, of 'Elephant Man' fame.

This view disappeared in 1938, when the western wing of the Royal Baths was built on the site of the demolished Winter Gardens and rockery. The little building at right which contained the entrance and waiting room to the Peat baths, is Harrogate's last surviving Edwardian Spa building, as well as its least known. Behind a commonplace exterior may be found a jewel of an interior, with glorious glass, plaster and woodwork, including the finest doorcase in Harrogate. The townspeople will do well to ensure that this is preserved. [Supplied by Mr S. Townson]

The old Council Chambers

Here is a view of the upper central portion of the New Victoria Baths as they appeared in about 1905, complete with the famous tree which stood in the middle of the road, but which nobody wanted to cut down. The view is unusual because it was the normal practice of photographers to take a picture of the whole length of the building, including two end pavilions which housed the baths for men and for women. The baths had been built in 1871 to a design which officially was by the town's surveyor, James Richardson, but which in reality was the result of Richardson having scrutinised plans submitted by various architects, including the celebrated Bown and Hiscoe.

It seems that Richardson failed to explain to the architects involved, that the plans would be deemed to be the property of the Improvement Commissioners, once they were handed in. A total premium of £130 was paid for the three best schemes by Bown, Dyson and Hiscoe, after which Richardson took the best aspects of each design and re-submitted as his own. Today, such behaviour would constitute a breach of copyright, but in 1871 it was acceptable practice! The foundation stone was laid by Richard Ellis on 4 February 1871, shortly before a particularly dirty election campaign, in which Ellis – the best public servant Harrogate has ever had – lost his seat. The Victoria Baths, as they were called, were opened on 26 August 1871, with a gala in the Spa Rooms.

The upper storey of the central block contained space for the Improvement Commissioners, as this body had outgrown the available space in the Old Town Hall in Swan Road; today the Mercer Art Gallery. The Victoria Baths were converted into the present Municipal Buildings in 1930-31, and it is interesting to reflect that the town's elected representatives have, since 1871, met in the same space – admittedly not much by York standards, but a respectable enough time nevertheless. [Supplied by Mr S. Townson]

On seeing this photograph of old St Mary's Church, St Mary's Walk, declared unsafe in 1904, and finally dismantled in 1923, the author was reminded of some of the stories which used to circulate about the vicar, Ralph Bates Hunter. He frequently went without breeches, having a long black overall coat which came below his knees, with black garters below.

Being in this state one Sunday, he took the following as his text: 'Brethren – there are three things of which I should speak to you – one that you know not – one that I know not – and one that none of us know. The first is I am without breeches, of which you know not; the second is what you will all give me towards a new pair, I know not; the third is what yon rogue of a tailor will charge for making them, none of us know!' Reverend Hunter sermonised most eloquently on the evils of drink, and no doubt in order to get to know the enemy spent most of his time in the inns of Harrogate. On one occasion, the vicar, in the company of his clerk, an old soak called Harry Buck, were drinking at an inn near the church, when Buck, being drunk, fell asleep.

The parson, being wide awake, and a practical joker, at once took off his clerk's shoes, and threw them into the fire, and then, being overcome with the fumes and strong drink, fell asleep. After a while, the clerk awoke, and on discovering his loss and who had been responsible, instantly retaliated by consigning the sleeping parson's shoes into the same fire, where they shared a like fate to his own. Another time, the vicar had been drinking most of the week, stopping day and night in a public house near Pannal Ash (now gone). When Sunday came round, he was awakened by the landlord from a drunken sleep, with: "Mr Hunter, it's Sunday morning and nearly nine o'clock." "Thou does not say so, does thee?" cried the drowsy parson. "Oh, but it is, I'll assure ye," returned the landlord. "Why then", said the Vicar, "thou mun send your Bill down to auld Bet and tell her to send th'top sarmon oop."

Reverend Hunter lodged in a small cottage near the Sulphur Well, nicely placed between the Bell Inn and the Promenade Inn, where he kept 52 sermons in a pile, reading them in rotation, placing the last one at the bottom of the pile. The landlord's boy did as he was bid, collected the top sermon from old Bet – who may well have been Betty Lupton, the 'Queen of the Wells' – and the sermon was delivered in the usual manner.

Isaac Greenbury's Pantheon

The building at the corner of James Street and the cross-James Street link to Market Place, has undergone several transformations since being opened on 31 August 1851 as a Methodist Chapel for central Harrogate – soon to be known as the Victoria Park. Richard Ellis was a prominent trustee, and when the James Street Salem Chapel became too small for the growing population, Ellis built the great Victoria Park Methodist Chapel, giving the land in the process. Sunwin House now stands on the site.

The earlier building proved more long lived, for shortly after the opening of the larger chapel, the James Street building was converted into commercial premises for the Whitby Jet ornament manufacturer, Isaac Greenbury, who had been born in Whitby in 1815. It is known that Greenbury exhibited his work at the Crystal Palace exhibition in 1851, and that he supplied the Empress of France and the Queen of Bavaria with examples of his art. He appears to have moved to Harrogate in the mid-1850s, with premises at Park Terrace, and Parliament Street, before settling in James Street. Whitby Jet became especially popular as an ornament of mourning, following the death of Prince Albert in 1861, and the rapidly developing

town of Harrogate must have been a magnet for an enterprising man of business such as Isaac Greenbury. In the accompanying photograph, Isaac Greenbury's shop – the Pantheon – is shown with the proud proprietor, sporting mutton-chop whiskers and a top hat, standing at extreme left.

To his right may be seen another top-hatted man, said to be Harrogate's stationmaster. Greenbury crossed swords with Harrogate's notorious pugilistic photographer, Hiram Compton Booth, who not only assaulted dissatisfied customers with dismaying regularity, but also indulged in a stream of useless civil cases, most of which he lost. Greenbury accused Booth of embezzlement in the matter of a picture deal, which resulted in Booth being sentenced to three months hard labour at Leeds assizes. At far left may be seen the entrance to the garden, which was later the site of Walter Davey's photographic studio. Towards the end of the century, the Pantheon was converted into the King's Arcade, running through to Market Place, and today, it contains the business of Richard Shops. Some of the above information has been kindly supplied to the author by Mr White, a descendant of the Greenbury's.

The old Dragon Barn

This extraordinary photograph of what is now Oxford Street in central Harrogate, was taken in about 1862 at a time when the Victoria Park Company was developing the open fields between High and Low Harrogate. At far right, two men are engaged in a conversation more or less where, some 40 years later, the entrance to the Harrogate Theatre would be built. The field behind them had been reserved for the construction of the new Cheltenham Parade, with the best site being set aside for the Primitive Methodist Chapel designed by Arthur Hiscoe and erected in 1872.

This Chapel was converted into the Empire Music Hall in 1911, and today it houses a splendid Italian restaurant, Pinocchio's. To the left, the Bower Street railway arch may be seen. This arch had collapsed in dramatic circumstances during the construction work of 1861, but was quickly rebuilt, prior to the opening of the new Central Railway Station in 1862. Beneath the embankment may be seen the footpath which marked the boundary of the future Lower Station Parade. Beyond the railway line lay Dragon Fields, which belonged to the farm of the great Dragon Hotel. The large building of Dragon Barn may easily be seen at centre right. Dragon Barn had been a childhood haunt of one of Harrogate's most famous citizens, the great painter William Powell Frith.

A public footpath ran along side the barn, and after dark, it was said to be difficult to get children to pass it, for the common knowledge told that Dragon Barn was haunted by a hob. Eventually, Dragon Barn fell victim to the changes which converted open fields into a busy commercial area, and the Dragon Estate was built on the site of the farm.

Sequah, and the Italian Gardens

In May 1891, a photographer took this view of the junction of Beulah Street and Cambridge Street, including at right the row of single-storey shops which are still in existence. At left may be seen the handsome portico that was the entrance to the St James's Coffee House and Conservative Club. The portico was demolished a few years later in order to enable vehicles to enter Beulah Street, but the building survives. Beyond the hoarding were a few cottages, fronted by an open area, which, for some reason, was given the name of the Italian Gardens. This was the favourite pitch of one of old Harrogate's most colourful characters, Sequah, who had arrived in town in *c.*1887.

A tall man, about 35 years of age, Sequah had long black shining hair, an aquiline nose, high cheek-bones, with a costume of heavily fringed buck-skins, gaudy neckerchief, and a grey floppy hat with a high crown and wide brim. From a platform atop a horse-drawn wagon, and banging a large drum, Sequah travelled round the town, announcing that he was a north American Indian, possessed of special powers of curing ailments. On his arrival at the Italian Gardens in Beulah Street, the side of the wagon would be let down, and business would then

commence. Sequah would hold up a bottle of Sequah's Prairie Flower cordial, which was guaranteed to cure any ailment – none of your modern nonsense about different cures for different ailments – gout, rheumatism, indigestion, toothache: Prairie Flower cordial cured the lot. Sequah was also famous for his painless dentistry, which he practised on those foolish people who had failed to drink enough of his cordial which guaranteed to prevent toothache!

For these special sessions, Sequah hired a military band, which gathered in a semi-circle around his wagon, Sufferers with bad teeth were invited up on to the wagon, where they sat in a chair, with mouths as wide as they could make them. The band struck up loudly, Sequah seized a pair of forceps, and during an especially percussive musical passage, would extract the offending tooth. The extractions were carried out at the rate of two a minute, and without any anaesthetic, and the noise of the band helped drown out the cries of the customers. After all the bad teeth had been extracted – for which Sequah never made any charge – the wagon, with Sequah on top, and accompanied by the band, moved off towards his lodgings in Princes Street.

Valley Gardens
100 years ago

This delightful and evocative photograph, taken about 100 years ago, shows children in the Valley Gardens, gazing towards one of the water features. The footpath at left is the old route leading from the Sulphur Well to the Bogs Field, recognised as a public right of way by the Award of 1778. It remained in a primitive condition until the *Harrogate Advertiser* opened a campaign in June 1850 for the gravelling of the footpath and the planting of shrubs along its edges. The campaign was aimed at the Harrogate Improvement Commissioners, and the *Advertiser* commented frequently on the slow rate of progress made in the areas enhancement. In 1852, the *Advertiser* reported that the stiles between the Old Well and the Bogs Field had been replaced with turnstiles, and that the authorities were promising to improve the footpath, which on rainy days took on the appearance of a marsh. Months went by without any improvements, and the letters page of the *Advertiser* was filled with comments from the public, giving their opinions of the commissioners in no uncertain manner.

One of the difficulties was that Bogs Field itself was part of the Stray, the herbage of which was then controlled by a number of so-called 'Stray-Gate' owners, who could see no advantage in improving footpaths across land which they used to depasture cattle. However, in 1854, the Commissioners greatly improved access to the wells of Bogs Field. A number of stone well-heads were constructed, using the old pyramid shape which may still be seen in prints of the area, or indeed in surviving examples at Haverah Park. At far right, a rare view of Valley Drive before David Simpson began building the splendid terraces which today form such an effective architectural backdrop to the gardens.

Promenade Square

Today, the name Well Hill is generally given to the point at which Cornwall Road joins Swan Road, where a number of handsome 18th-century houses overlook the Royal Pump Room and its Old Sulphur Well. However, in the early 19th century, the area had more of the character of a square, as the present entrance to Valley Gardens was filled with houses, and the Old Sulphur Well had not received the bulky structure of the Royal Pump Room. The name Promenade Square came from the most prominent feature of the square, the old Promenade Inn, which still stands at the corner of Swan Road and Crescent Road.

This photograph of 1912 shows the western side of Promenade Square with its three large houses. The first, at far left, was called 'Roseville', and in the early years of the 19th century, it was occupied by Mrs Clayton, a widow, who had in her husband's time been landlady of the Bell Inn on Royal Parade. She sold the Bell on 30 November 1815, retiring to Roseville on the proceeds. Widow Clayton appears to have been a friend of Betty Lupton, the 'Queen of the Wells', and no doubt the two friends did not refrain from voicing their opinions on the changing face of Harrogate! Next door to Widow Clayton was Major

Thackwray's Lodging House. Major (this was his Christian name) Thackwray was related to the famous Thackwray's of the Crown Hotel, and he also worked as a mason at the Mount Pleasant Stone Quarry, where the Grand Hotel – now Windsor House – was built.

The next house was occupied by one of Regency Harrogate's most famous characters, Nanny Anson, a kindly and apparently childless woman who provided a most useful service as a childminder. Nanny Anson looked after the infants of those wealthy, pleasure-seeking families who wished to enjoy Harrogate's high life, without the encumbrance of small children. The children of local working families, including those of hotel staff, were also placed in her keeping. Nanny Anson was famed for her soothing cordial – the recipe for which has not survived, but which probably included liberal doses of gin and laudanum! – which late-19th century reminiscences claimed could quiet the most fractious child. This photograph was taken during the construction of an improved entrance to Valley Gardens. The houses were then owned by Harrogate Corporation, but were not demolished until the early 1930s.

Occasionally, photographs of old Harrogate appear, which can not be identified with precision, and such a one is shown here. Marked 'Sevastopol celebrations, Harrogate Stray', the photograph shows a number of military cannons, surrounded by children and adults. In September 1855, the people of Harrogate were given a respite from grumbling about the failings – real or imagined – of the Improvement Commissioners, turning instead to consider a piece of international news, the fall of the Russian city of Sevastopol, or Sebastopol, as it is sometimes spelled. The Harrogate newspapers had carried full reports of the Crimean War, between allies Great Britain and France, one the one hand, and Russia on the other.

The allied siege of Sevastopol – including the disastrous Charge of the Light Brigade – had been the subject of much comment in the *Advertiser* and *Herald*, so the Harrogate public were well briefed when news came through that Sevastopol had fallen to the allies on 9 September. The news was greeted with near-delirium in town, with High and Low Harrogate each vying with one another, to see which could produce the most spectacular street decorations. A grand procession was arranged, which marched though High and Low Harrogate. There was a Royal Salute with 21 guns. The Stray in front of the Crown Hotel was laid out with tables, on which a

dinner of good old English fare, at three o'clock was provided for the townspeople. A leaflet advised: 'The labouring classes – knifes, forks, and plates provided – each man to bring his own appetite.'

After dinner, a programme of rural sports was staged donkey races, bell races, foot races, jumping-in-sack races; greased poles were set up, with those managing to climb to the top winning a sucking pig; there were also wheelbarrow races down Cold Bath Lane, and a number of water-filled barrels provided for apple-ducking competitions. After the singing of the National Anthem, the crowd climbed Montpellier Hill to where a replica of a Russian 'Malakhoff Tower' had been constructed. The crowd, which numbered about 8,000, then witnessed the climax of the celebrations, as an assault was made on the tower, which was filled with combustible materials. After a terrific bombardment with mortars and rockets, the tower went up in flames, numerous members of the crowd discharged firearms, and – accompanied by the bells of old St Mary's Church – mass cheering broke out, with three cheers each for Queen Victoria, Prince Albert, and the Emperor of France.

It was all horribly dangerous, and great fun. It seems that Sevastopol Day was commemorated in Harrogate on several later occasions, and this photograph may record one such celebration towards the end of the 1880s

The old Toffee Shop

Farrah's Harrogate Toffee Shop in pictured here in its earliest location in Crescent Road. Harrogate Toffee – in the author's opinion the best toffee in the world – was invented in the 1830s by a man called Swan. Swan was a grocer with a shop directly opposite the Old Sulphur Well, and was therefore ideally placed to supply water drinkers with sweet meats to remove the taste of some of the town's stronger mineral waters. According to the memories of the late W. H. Breare, published on 4 January 1893, Swan was 'an adept at fruit wines, and the cellar of the old Promenade Room (today, the Mercer Art Gallery) contained quantities in bottle of his most expert preparations. Mr Farrah was an assistant with Mr Swan, and his elder sister was also identified with the business. They succeeded to the original Harrogate Toffee recipe, and have held undisputed possession ever since. Mr Farrah speaks with very great admiration of his old master. He considered him one of the cleverest men in his own line he had ever met...'

Sometime later, Farrah's acquired premises across the road in Royal Parade, which closed only in January 1999, when the business was bought by Mr Gary Marston and incorporated with his Montpellier Parade Chocolate Shop. This delightful postcard shows Farrah's original premises in Crescent Road, built between the old Promenade Inn at far left, and the even older Crescent Inn, at far right. [Supplied by Mrs Lunn]

An aerial view of Queen Ethelburga's School, *c.*1950.

A solitary motor vehicle disturbs the peace of Starbeck High Street, 1910.

Benches at the junction of Leeds Road and Langcliffe Avenue enabled residents to watch the interesting new phenomenon of motor traffic, *c.*1910.

Parliament Street, with its wide pavements and elegant street canopies, welcomed pedestrians in all weather.

The meet of the Bramham Moor Fox hounds, outside the Old Swan Hotel, *c.19*60.

Farrah's Cafe, Royal Parade, provided first rate views of Crown Place and the Royal Pump Room.

The Prince of Wales Hotel

An uncommon view, *c*.1909, of the former Prince of Wales Hotel, which is today Prince of Wales Mansions. It seems that an inn had existed here from about 1815, as an advertisement placed by Michael Hattersley – many years waiter at the Granby – begged leave to inform the public that he had opened an hotel at the crossroads. This inn was on land which had been allotted under the great Award of 1778 to one Samuel Hatterley – or Hattersley, as the variant spelling recorded – and Michael may have been his son.

The inn was well placed to serve travellers on the busy turnpike roads to Leeds, Ripon and York, and it appears to have been one of the old coaching inns of the type so loved by Charles Dickens. The Wordsworths stayed here during their visits to Harrogate of 1823 and 1827, and indeed Mary Wordsworth wrote to a friend that if they came to Harrogate next year, they might take lodgings, which would be cheaper than the cost of Hattersley's establishment. At this time a coach left the Crossroads

Inn daily for Leeds and Ripon, and by 1837, the Union coach advertised that it also ran from the inn since – 1830 renamed the Brunswick. The hotel was well placed to serve the visitors arriving at Harrogate from the so-called Brunswick Railway Line, which opened a station directly opposite the hotel in 1848, more or less on the site of the present Trinity Church.

There is a delightful account of coaching scenes at the old Brunswick Hotel which was first published in the *Barnsley Times* in 1874, written possibly by one of the Carter Brothers: "Visitors in the town gathered at the Brunswick corner at about four o'clock to gaze up the Leeds Road for the distant cloud of white dust which heralded the approach of the 'mail'. What excitement there was, and anxiety to catch the first glimpses of the leading bays, what anticipations for expected friends, what a perennial joy was the bright toot of the pleasant horn, and the first wave from the wee laddie perched up atop among the 'outsides', and then the jingle-jingle of the brasses and harness, the steaming horses, the cheery welcomes…"

The broad terrace known as 'Pier Head', or Prospect Promenade, provided an agreeable observation platform over Low Harrogate.

The Sun Pavilion provided an oasis of peace in the wartime world of 1940.

The Winter Gardens Terrace

The Royal Baths Winter Gardens, seen from an unusual angle, with the tower of the Crown Hotel in the background, and the entrance to the Peat Baths at far left. The land on which the Royal Baths stand, had been acquired by the corporation in 1888, when they purchased the old Montpellier Baths, which had originally been part of the Crown Hotel estate, which at the beginning of the 19th century had encompassed all the land between Parliament Street, Crescent Road, Montpellier Road, and the Ginnel.

This is an area of Harrogate which probably contains more mineral springs than any other area, save for that miracle of nature, the Bogs Field, in Valley Gardens. Long before the Montpellier Baths were built in 1834, the field was used to pasture horses of guests staying at the Crown Hotel. According to the reminiscences of some elderly Harrogate residents, published in the *Advertiser* in the 1890s, it was their habit as children to cross Crown Field on their way to school at Miss Parry's academy in Strawberrydale, when they would look out for shining pools of sulphur water which gathered in the hoof marks left by horses in the soft ground. In the 1820s, Joseph Thackwray sunk some wells in Crown Field, meeting with great success, and eventually, he built the little Chinese Pump Room, which was swept away when the Royal Baths were built after 1894. [Supplied by Mr S. Townson]

Royal Hall Gardens

was particularly beloved by generations of Harrogate children – Peter Pan. After the Rose Gardens were destroyed to make way for the Exhibition Halls, Peter Pan was re-sited in Valley Gardens, but was subsequently damaged by vandals. This is sad, as there is something quintessentially Edwardian about Peter Pan, the same being true for Valley Gardens. Beautiful as the Rose Gardens were, the Exhibition Halls have been of greater significance for the success of post-war Harrogate's economic life. The first exhibition hall was put up in 1958, at the urgings of Mr Bill Baxter, costing £2,000, and built by Octavius Atkinson. Forty years on, there is talk that the H.I.C. will one day have to rebuild these 'temporary' exhibition halls from the 1950s and 1960s. Let the following suggestion therefore be given serious consideration: build new exhibition halls with roof gardens, which could stretch the length of King's Road from the junction with Cheltenham Crescent.

Such roof gardens could be connected to the grounds of the Hotel Majestic, and form a fine amenity for conference and exhibition delegates, as well as the general public. They could be reached from the exhibition halls below by means of escalators, and would be a unique feature in the world of exhibiting. Harrogate must not redevelop the old exhibition halls in a piece-meal manner, especially with regard to traffic considerations, but must have the courage to look to the site in its entirety, and think big. [Supplied by Mr S. Townson]

Bearing a 1928 franking, this postcard shows the Rose Gardens, which until 1959 stretched along King's Road, behind the Royal Hall. They had originally been part of the much larger gardens of the former Spa Rooms, laid out after 1835, and remodelled in the early 1870s. Before the Valley Gardens saw much development, the Spa Room Gardens were regarded as being the finest in Harrogate, and were hugely popular with visitors. At far right may be seen the fine railings marking the King's Road boundary, whilst in the centre background gleams the white marble statue of Cupid & Psyche, which now takes pride of place in Crescent Gardens.

The other statue, at lower right, was a statue which

Royal Hall Gardens and Hotel Majestic

The Hotel Majestic was only four years old when this splendid postcard view was taken. The interesting thing about the card is not the view of the Majestic, which is a famous Harrogate landmark, but rather the view of the little-photographed northern boundary of the Royal Hall Gardens.

The boundary between the Majestic grounds and those of the Royal Hall estate, is hidden by the foliage which bisects the site from left to right. Two features are visible in this photograph of *c*.1902 – a little rustic shelter, of the kind once so common in Harrogate's parks and gardens, and a curious square stone building, crowned by a battlement, and fronted with a stout gothic door. The latter feature may have been an ornamental 'folly', built to provide the grounds with an interesting *point de vue*, or it could have been a pumphouse, to contain one of the site's innumerable iron springs.

Prospect Cottage – Milan Coffee House

This extraordinary view of what is now Oxford Street, taken from Parliament Street in about 1865 from the position now filled by the Nationwide Building Society, shows at right the magnificent classical frontage of the Wesleyan Methodist Chapel, then only three years old. At left may be seen part of a much older property, Prospect Cottage, which may have been the principal residence of the medieval Crokesnab, the lands of which separated the two villages of High and Low Harrogate.

In 1810, the whole of the farm land between what is now King's Road and York Place – virtually the entire business centre of the modern town – was bought for £9,000 by a shrewd speculator, James Franklin, who gave his name to both James Street and the later Franklin estate. Prospect Cottage was then the only substantial building standing between the two locations, enjoying an unbroken view south as far as York Place. It became Franklin's home in 1814, where he lived until his death in 1826, when it passed to his daughter.

The carriage road connecting Prospect Cottage to Parliament Street may still be seen in the form of the arch and road at the top of Parliament Street. Eventually, the estate was bought by George Dawson, who began developing Cambridge Crescent in 1867, after which Prospect Cottage disappeared from view, it being commonly accepted that it had been demolished. However, in 1995 when the commercial premises in Oxford Street were refurbished for a coffee house, it was found that the chore of the buildings included virtually the whole of Prospect Cottage, which – like similar buildings in York – had been submerged by later, 19th-century buildings. The south front of what is undoubtedly the oldest surviving structure in central Harrogate, may now been seen from the pleasant courtyard of Milan's Coffee House, an interesting relic of the time when it was the only building between King's Road and York Place.

All Saints' Church, Harlow Hill

Postcards with photographs of Harrogate cemeteries are rare, since few of us would relish receiving one from a friend marked 'wish you were here'. Yet here is an interesting specimen, which shows All Saints' Church and Cemetery on Harlow Hill, *c*.1915. The Church had been built in 1870 to serve the spiritual needs of parishioners of the outlying district of St Mary's, and the land for both church and cemetery had – most generously – been given to the town by the Earl of Harewood. Although in recent times we have all read about the splendid developments at the newer Stonefall Cemetery, which indeed forms a most beautiful and useful ornament to the town, there are many in Harrogate who are deeply alarmed at the state of our other local cemeteries.

This is always a sensitive matter to discuss, as the authorities responsible for the upkeep of our cemeteries have their resources stretched to the utmost, and are usually as keenly aware of shortcomings as their most vociferous critics. Perhaps it is time to establish a 'Friends of Harrogate Cemeteries', similar to the 'Friends of York Cemetery', which under the guidance of appropriate authorities, provides volunteers to maintain the grounds, repair damage and organise educational events. Under this last heading come talks about famous people buried in the cemetery, the wildlife of cemeteries, histories of churches and graveyards, the art of cemeteries, and many other topics which attract audience interest.

Parliament Street and Mincing Lane

Parliament Street's once wide pavements are seen in this card which shows Exchange Buildings at the corner of the Ginnel. The former Exchange Public House, an establishment which, if memory serves correctly, had acquired an 'interesting' reputation by the time of its closure in the 1970s! The Exchange Block had been built for site owners Richardson and Thwaites from 1870 to 1876, as a speculative development of shops, spirit vaults and billiard saloon, the latter, now the Harrogate Antiques Centre, being reached by means of a bridge at first-floor level. One hundred years later, the block had been so neglected as to make it the subject of a massive plan of redevelopment, which called for the demolition of Exchange Buildings, and all other Parliament Street properties up to and including the Somerset Hotel – now Yates' Wine Lodge.

These demolitions were necessary for the realisation of a proposal to build an immense supermarket for Morrison. Try to imagine, reader, if you have strong nerves, the state of Parliament Street today if this proposal had been achieved. Mincing Lane, seen at right, ran down to the back of the Exchange, running parallel to the old public footpath, the Ginnel, which connects Low Harrogate to High Harrogate. When this photograph was taken, the Ginnel was restricted to pedestrian use, as shown by the position of the large ornamental lamppost, which straddles the present vehicular exit point. [Supplied by Mr George Fowler]

Prince of Wales corner c.1912

The Prince of Wales Hotel, extended considerably to the east in 1898, owes its origins to a successful coaching inn established in Regency times at the important junction of the Ripon and Leeds turnpike road with the Otley to Knaresborough turnpike road. This view of *c*.1912 shows the busy junction being controlled by a police constable. Traffic at this time was becoming something of an irritant, and motorists were liable to a stiff fine of 20 shillings if caught indulging in 'racing' – especially if Alderman Fortune was on the bench, who regarded ten miles per hour as outrageous.
[Supplied by Mr George Fowler]

Novelty cards

From time to time, a few old Harrogate postcards turn up with novelty or humour for their subject. Before World War One, the series photographed by Mark Mitchell achieved great popularity, featuring the efforts of a small boy in sampling the water of the Old Sulphur Well. Today, such images may appear unduly coy, as taste has changed since the time of their publication in 1908. They are nevertheless worth reproducing, not only because of the insight they provide into Edwardian humour, but also because their high quality and clarity reveals much detail. The first of six such cards shows a small boy standing on the wide pavement of Royal Parade, clutching a newspaper, holding a pipe in his mouth, and saying: "Good morning – will you sulphur with me?"

Across the narrow road may be seen the Royal Pump Room, in front of which is the temporary ticket office and temporary annex. These two structures had been provided to ease crowding at the Royal Pump Room, which on a good day could record as many as 1,000 drinkers. Their temporary nature is explained by the fact that the Council could not make up its mind about whether or not to build a proper extension on to the old Royal Pump Room, or to demolish the old building and start from scratch. In the event, they decided to construct a light-weight iron and glass annex, which was opened in 1913 by the Lord Mayor of London, by which time it appears that these novelty postcards were still selling. [Supplied by Mr S. Townson]

Low Harrogate, 1820

Low Harrogate in a print of about 1820, the artist having taken a position on the Stray on Montpellier Hill that is more or less equivalent today to one opposite the Blues Bar on Montpellier Hill. Allowance must be made for artistic licence, but the scene, on the whole is an accurate representation of the centre of Sulphur Wells, as Low Harrogate was then known. At far left, the long white stucco structure of the old White Hart, showing at left the two storeyed wing containing the long room, and at right, the side road which led to the rear stables. Separated from the White Hart by this side road, and a pair of poplar trees, the Bell Inn is then shown, together with its neighbouring lodging house and shop.

This little cluster of buildings hides the structure of the Promenade Coaching Office, which was located at the foot of what is now Valley Drive. Surrounded by the inns of Low Harrogate, the coaching office was well located for visitors staying at the White Hart, the Bell, the Crown, the Crescent, and the Promenade

(neither of which are shown here) as well as the Lodging Houses of Well Hill. After the 1840s, the Bell Inn and the coaching office were incorporated into the developing Royal Parade. At centre may be seen the dome of the temple which since 1807 had covered the Old Sulphur Well. This was replaced in 1842 with the present Royal Pump Room, the old temple being removed to High Harrogate to cover the Tewit Well. The still surviving buildings on Well Hill may be seen above the dome of the Well, which is then flanked at right by the Crown Hotel, then the greatest of the Low Harrogate inns.

To the right of this is seen part of Ashfield House, which the Thackwray's built as an overflow, or lodging house, for their Crown Hotel. The boundary wall of Ashfield House garden runs up Montpellier Hill at far right, more or less following the line of Montpellier Parade, develop by George Dawson after 1860. The two posts on the Stray mark the junction of what is now the entrance to Montpellier Street, with the Stray. [Supplied by Mrs E. Hewick]

Tewit Well – the nation's oldest Spa

Doubtless the citizens of Bath are rejoicing over recent news that their city is to receive liberal funding from the Millennium Fund to further assist the continuing story of their Spa's revival. Doubtless. Such funding should also be applied to England's oldest Spa, still slumbering in utter neglect, as are the St John's Well, the Magnesia Well and the Kissingen Well – to name only three. In case readers may not be aware of the significance of the Tewit Well – seen here in about 1860 – it is worth recalling something of its history.

This well, discovered by Mr William Slingsby, in 1571, was the very first mineral well in England to be given the name of Spa long before the noun was applied to Bath. It was praised by no less a person than Dr Timothy Bright, personal physician to both Queen Elizabeth and Lord Burghley. It was the subject of one of the most important Spa treatises ever written, Edmund Deane's *Spadacrene Anglica* of 1626. It was of all mineral wells in England the one with the longest record of continual use for drinking, as recommended by the medical profession, and – until its closure by Harrogate Council in 1971 – could record no less than 400 years of public access. Today, it is so neglected that the very well itself has been lost, being a few yards from the Tewit Well temple of 1807.

Surely, if anything in Harrogate is worth heritage funding, it is England's oldest Spa.

Hankey-pankey in the woods!

It is possible to ascribe much of the commercial success of old Harrogate to the fact that the majority of Councillors were shrewd businessmen who were versed equally in the art of making money as well as spending it. Throughout the 19th and early 20th centuries, there appears to have been an unwritten understanding that Harrogate's best interest lay in attracting visitors who had the means to enjoy long visits to the town, thus keeping the hotels, shops, and other businesses on a firm and regular financial basis.

Day visitors, or 'trippers' were undesirable, as the majority tended to arrive in trains or charabancs, make use of the expensive parks and gardens laid out for the wealthy visitors but freely open to all, consume food and drink brought into town rather than purchased in local shops, and behave in a manner somewhat beneath the exalted view that the town had of itself. It is, possibly, for these reasons that local businesses selling Harrogate picture postcards,

preferred to stock views of imposing public buildings, parks and gardens, or of elegant people walking through the town's streets.

Postcards of vulgar subjects were not encouraged, and although the public could often buy pictures of what to modern taste must seem cloying or sentimental matter, the Harrogate equivalent of the saucy seaside postcard does not seem to have existed. All of which makes this view of Harlow Woods all the more interesting. The card is entitled 'The force of example', made for 'Bilton's P.C. Emporium' and photographed by J. Welch and Sons of Portsmouth; the colour card was printed in Belgium. Four couples are shown enjoying each others company in the not-very-private area of Harlow Moor. The card seems to have been purchased by a young man lodging at 8 Cheltenham Mount, who sent it to a lady friend with the message: 'It would be much better (*i.e. in Harrogate*) if it was like the other side of this p.c., 28 July 1908.' [Supplied by Mr D. Hird]

Tree planting on the Stray

The first serious attempt to beautify the fringes of the Stray through the planting of trees took place in the 1860s, when the Improvement Commissioners planted saplings along the main turnpike roads into Harrogate: Skipton Road, York Place, West Park and Leeds Road. There appears to have been an understanding that whenever there arose a public demand for trees on the streets of the town, the Commissioners would provide the saplings, provided that the public provided the iron railings necessary for their protection.

It was understood by all, that saplings attracted vandals, and that if the saplings were to survive, it was necessary to provide them with tree-guards of the type shown in this photograph of West Park Stray. As it was also understood that railings were more expensive than saplings, it was usual to raise the cost of the railings before that of the saplings. During the last 20 years of the 20th century, a number of intensive programmes of tree planting took place on the Stray, which threatened to alter the traditional open nature of the 'world's biggest lawn', dividing it up with tree-lined paths. Do the townspeople really want to lose the great open expanse of the Stray? Perhaps alternative sites should be considered, such as Bilton, Starbeck and Jennyfield. Keep the remaining open Stray open.

Traffic management King's Road, 1912

A constable controls traffic at the junction of King's Road, with Parliament Street and Ripon Road, in this photograph of *c.*1912. The female pedestrians. all carry parasols in protection from the summer sun, to guard their skins from acquiring an unfashionably swarthy sun tan. The canopies of Parliament Street, at right, will provide welcome relief for those without protection

The constable turns to see an oncoming cyclist, just passing the entrance of the Spa Hotel – now Jimmy's Night Club – then only ten years old. At left, the southern façade of the Spa Rooms, and the magnificent row of Beech trees which, until 1911, formed the southern boundary of the Spa Rooms Gardens. In 1911, Mr W. H. Baxter of Harrogate donated money to pay for the improvement of King's Road, including shifting the old boundary of the Spa Rooms garden, to a more northerly site, which enabled a fine pavement to be constructed along the north side of King's Road. This new pavement incorporated the great row of Beech trees, which then made King's Road into one of the greenest and most attractive thoroughfares in Harrogate. However, in the 1970s and 1980s, as the site of the old gardens was converted for exhibition hall use, a strange thing began to happen. One by one, the trees were cut down. Nothing strange about that, as trees are always being cut down and replaced in Harrogate.

The strange thing about King's Road is that none of the trees were ever replaced. This gradual erosion went on – undisturbed – until by 1990 the whole avenue had been felled, being replaced with a mess of black tar paving. The vandals responsible for this shameful ruination have never been held to account for their actions.

Edwardian rush-hour traffic in the Station-forecourt c.1908

Even before World War One, Harrogate experienced problems with motor traffic, as may be seen here with the line of charabancs awaiting passengers in the Railway Station's forecourt. In the background may be seen the trees of Station Parade, behind which rise the premises of Pattison's, Chemists – which stood at the junction with Cambridge Street, demolished a few years ago for the Victoria Centre. At centre, the high gable of the Beulah Street Arcade – restored in 1997-98 for Argos Sports Intersport – and to the far right, the building now occupied by Bottoms Up! wine merchants. Motor charabancs were, for many years, not welcome in Harrogate, and the council actively discouraged their presence in the town.

They were regarded with particular horror by civic leaders such as Dr Myrtle, Alderman Simpson, and Alderman Fortune, who considered that they lowered the tone of the place by allowing the unwashed hordes from the industrial towns of Yorkshire, from Lancashire, and Tyneside, to descend on Harrogate, where they would disturb the pleasures of wealthy visitors.

This attitude was, in part, a relic from the days of the building of the railway into Harrogate, in the 1840s, when the opinion was expressed that a railway would be a disaster, as it would enable the 'lower orders' to flood into the town, without regard for the propriety of the visitors to the 'water cure', or the sanctity of the sabbath. In the 1893-94, the *Illustrated London News* published a series of superb drawings of Harrogate by Templar, which caricatured the town's reaction to 'trippers'. Even as late as 1930, a member of the Harrogate Chamber of Trade suggested that a doctor should be employed at Harrogate Station to turn away visitors who were not wealthy invalids. [Supplied by Mr D. Hird]

Benwell House

Benwell House, on Well Hill, Cornwall Road, was rarely the subject of a postcard view. To obtain an idea of its location, the viewer should stand on the Cornwall Road footpath which flanks Valley Gardens, so that the front of Promenade House on Well Hill is parallel to the front of the building in this picture. Benwell House was an 18th-century building, used to lodge visitors who preferred the more personal attentions of the owner, to the often impersonal lifestyles of the bigger hotels.

To modern ears, the name 'Lodging House' has a definite downmarket ring, but to earlier times, it was a term denoting exclusive and personal service. Hence the fine Georgian architecture, the tall rooms, and the commanding position overlooking the world famous Old Sulphur Well. In the early years of the 19th century, Benwell House was occupied by one of Harrogate's most colourful characters, Nanny Anson, who is referred to earlier. Nanny Anson was a childless woman who performed the socially useful role of childminder to those wealthy and pleasure seeking families visiting Harrogate, who wished to have a break from their parental duties. Nanny Anson was famed for her soothing cordial, which, it was said, would quiet the most fractious child. The recipe has not survived, but doubtless included liberal portions of gin and laudenum. In 1900 the Council decided to buy up all the remaining houses between Valley Gardens and Cornwall Road, including Benwell House, which were demolished after World War One.

A well of remarkable mineral water was discovered beneath Benwell House, and was subsequently analysed by Arnold Woodmansey, the borough analysist, who found that although it contained neither sulphide, nor more than a trace of iron, it had twice the rate of sulphate of any other Harrogate well, making it unique among the town's waters. The ramp which ran down to this forgotten well appears to have been filled in with earth in the 1970s, being behind the benches at the Valley Gardens entrance.

The Wellington Hotel

The establishment which was the Wellington Hotel was much older than the building which for so long bore the name of the famous Iron Duke. Cold Bath Road has a long history of association with the coaching trade, and the Wellington appears to have enjoyed its most colourful period during the first half of the 19th century, when such coaches as the *Alexander,* the *Dart,* or the *Emerald* would roll up amidst clouds of dust, steaming horses and jingling brass, to disgorge their passengers into the welcoming arms of the landlords of the many inns. The Wellington was known originally as the Robin Hood, but changed its name in honour of the victor of Waterloo. Built for George Harper, a member of one of Cold Bath Road's oldest – and most numerous – families, the Wellington appears to have been enlarged in the 1850s, before being completely rebuilt towards the end of the 19th century.

In 1822, the landlord, Joseph Cullingworth, used to charge five shillings a day for board and lodging. This photograph, lent by *Advertiser* reader David Hird, shows the Wellington when it was still an hotel, and with its superb decorative iron canopy still in place over the front door – a canopy which has sadly been removed, although its brother at the side of the building, may still be seen. Requisitioned in September 1939, the Wellington served as a hostel for civil servants employed in the various General Post Office departments established in Harrogate, and was converted into flats in 1953. Readers should look up to see the fine statue of the Duke of Wellington, which still gazes out across Cold Bath Road.

The Stray Hotel

The great Award of 1778, which followed the enclosure of the former Royal Forest of Knaresborough, allotted a portion of land in Harrogate between Otley Road and Cold Bath Road, to the Crown, through the Duchy of Lancaster. This land, known as the Red Bank Estate, was after 1850 leased to builders by the Duchy, who insisted that a high standard of construction be practised. In consequence, a number of fine villas were erected along what later became Beech Grove and Byron Walk, including Beech Lodge, Beech Villa, and this structure, 'Auracaria', which is today part of Stray Towers.

The villa was converted into an hotel in 1885, and considerably enlarged in 1905 through the addition of an east wing. In 1912 it was acquired by the Stray Hotel and Hydro Ltd., a newly-formed company, whose directors were William Peacock, managing director of the Harrogate Grand Opera House, a Leeds Insurance broker, R. C. Hamilton, who in 1934 became Mayor of Harrogate, and two other local men.

The conversion to hotel use had entailed considerable alterations, including provision of a decorative cast-iron canopy.

This picture shows the building shortly after it was acquired by the Stray Hotel & Hydro Company. The author has never seen a view of 'Auracaria' before its conversion, but it must have been a fine sight, as the stone work of the principal façade, facing Byron Walk, is of the highest quality. In 1939, on the outbreak of war, the Stray Hotel was requisitioned by the Government, and occupied by the West Riding of Yorkshire's Agricultural Executive Committee. At the war's end in 1945, the Hotel Company decided to sell its property and go into liquidation. The following decade saw the building converted into 17 flats, including the former east wing, which sold so well that by 1960 a second, detached, block was built between 'Auracaria' and Victoria Road. The old name of 'Auracaria' is said to derive from a monkey puzzle tree which grew on the frontage.

Station Square numbers 9 & 11

Numbers 9-11 Station Square are seen here *c.*1880. The building had been erected shortly after 1865, after completion of the handsome terrace which fills the south side of James Street. Numbers 9 & 11 were designed by the great J. H. Hirst of Bristol, and built by Richard Ellis, who had also built the terrace, with its superb façade of brick and stone, and a beautiful ground -floor sequence of arched windows. Numbers 9 & 11 were skillfully designed to link the terrace to the much taller stone bulk of the Station Hotel, and the architect adjusts the eyes to different heights of the terrace and hotel by keeping the terrace's cornice height but increasing the pitch of the roof and providing a massive stone dormer window, crowned with a finely carved Yorkshire Rose.

Whereas the terrace is a beautiful mixture of brick and stone, the link building is entirely stone, and the ground floor was enriched by superb arched windows. The contrast was wrecked in the 20th century through the coatings of the upper sections of the façade with completely inappropriate layers of paint, removal of the decorative ironwork between the two first-floor bay windows, and the destruction of the ground-floor windows. However, in 1998, the upper parts of the façade were cleaned and repaired, revealing once again the lovely honey coloured stonework.

Kursaal Gardens

Whereas the majority of early views of the Kursaal – later known as the Royal Hall – depicted either the principal frontage on Ripon Road, or the glazed terrace at the building's rear, which overlooked the tennis courts, this postcard has a rare view of the north façade, facing the gardens of the Hotel Majestic. This portion of the surrounding gardens was built over in *c.*1939, when the Council realised that they had lost a valuable amenity for the Royal Hall the previous year, when the neighbouring Spa Rooms were demolished. Accordingly, they had to construct a hideous tin-roofed annex on the north side of the Royal Hall, where the Exhibition Hall 'F' was eventually built.

Freezing cold in winter and like a baking oven in summer, the annex was a tawdry replacement for both the Spa Rooms and the garden. Interestingly, the postcard appears to have been posted on 12 August 1914, the very day that an event of considerable musical importance occurred – the first provincial performance of Vaughan William's *London Symphony*. It is well-known that the first provincial performance of Elgar's *Second Symphony* took place in Harrogate, few musicians are aware of a similar premier of the second symphony of Elgar's great young contemporary, Ralph Vaughan Williams. Moreover, Vaughan Williams came to Harrogate to conduct his work, which was an outstanding success. [Supplied by Mr D. Hird]

Heatherdene

Heatherdene used to stand on the eastern side of Wetherby Road next to the grounds of Harrogate Football Club, and was built in response to a tragedy. On 16 June 1883, during a pantomime performance at the Victoria Hall, Sunderland, a cry of 'Fire!' produced a stampede, during which 183 children were suffocated or crushed to death. The fire had been a tiny one, and soon extinguished, the real harm having been caused because the fire doors only opened inwards, preventing proper escape. The sorrow felt in Sunderland was felt throughout the nation, and a subscription to build a convalescent home for sick children, was supported widely.

Eventually, the subscription committee decided to build the memorial home in Harrogate, which then was at the peak of its Victorian fame as 'the world's greatest spa', and, with nationwide support, the new Heatherdene Convalescent Home was opened in Wetherby Road on 15 September 1892 by Mrs Stansfield Richardson, Mayoress of Sunderland. Once the subscription money ran out, Heatherdene was taken over by Sunderland Royal Infirmary, later becoming a men's convalescent home, where many

miners were sent. During World War One, Heatherdene was run by the Grand Duchess George of Russia, as a hospital for wounded servicemen, and indeed the war memorial given to Harrogate by the Grand Duchess may still be seen on the Stray at the junction with Wetherby Road. At this period, the Matron assisting the Grand Duchess was Miss Mary Macrea, who joined the staff in 1918, and who served with great dedication until her death in 1931. Her successor, Miss H. Dodd, gave equally distinguished service to the institution.

With the coming of the National Health Service, Heatherdene became a convalescent home for women, and it was still in operation in the 1960s. The author has particular reason to think of Heatherdene with gratitude, for a decade before he was born, his own mother, a Sunderland girl, convalesced there in the 1930s, after a serious illness. Today, all that is left of Heatherdene is a handsome brass plaque, now in the Heatherdene Social Club on Lancaster Park Road, and two forlorn stone gateposts on Wetherby Road, one of which still carries, in fading letters, the name Heatherdene. [Card supplied by Mr C. Hopes]

Before Littlewoods and Boots – Cambridge Street 1919

Cambridge Street photographed *c.*1919, showing the site later occupied by Littlewoods and Boots. The buildings at far left and far right still stand, the former being a book and gift shop, the latter being the premises of the Midland Bank. At centre stands the dignified stone frontage of the former stables – later garage – of the Prospect Hotel, beyond which may be seen part of a paddock belonging to the same business. The photograph was taken shortly before the stable/garage was demolished to make way for the marvel of the age, a new 'super-cinema', the Scala, which opened on Monday, 4 October 1920. With 1,400 seats, the Scala was a great advance on the town's other cinemas.

Built in a heavy Palladian style, with a frontage of white glazed tiles, the Scala provided Cambridge Street with a structure of considerable character, the opening advertisement boasting 'the Scala undoubtedly achieves the premier position of any cinema playhouse in the Kingdom'. The Scala, which changed its name to Gaumont on 12 June 1950, must have raised the value of the neighbouring paddock, because by 1928 a new building had risen between the cinema and John Street. Built by the Harrogate Gas company at the same time as their development in neighbouring James Street, the new Cambridge Street building was tenanted by a variety of retailers – readers may recall a Wimpy Bar, and a chemists, on the site – until it was acquired by Boots, who, to their great credit, spent a considerable sum in restoring the handsome classical façade.

As for the cinema, it finally closed on 26 September 1959, with a performance of *Al Capone*, staring Rod Steiger, before suffering the indignity of demolition in 1962. This was a pity, as the cinema was so much a product of the 1920s, an era that, architecturally, is not well represented in Harrogate. And the present Littlewoods store is just a characterless box.

Victoria Hall, James Street

It may seem strange to recall that in the middle of the 19th century, James Street was home to two places of worship. One of them was Salem Chapel, built probably by Richard Ellis in 1851 to serve the Methodist residents of what later became Victoria Park. The building still stands, in considerably modified form, at the corner of James Street and cross-James Street, where it is occupied by Richard Shops. The other place of worship had originally been constructed in High Harrogate, being consecrated in 1749. This was St John's Church, precursor of the present Christ Church, which replaced St John's in 1831.

The fabric of the redundant St John's Church was purchased for £100 by the Harrogate Congregationalist movement, who were then worshipping at the so-called Cross Chapel at Smithy Hill which they were outgrowing. The Congregationalists dismantled St John's, and transported it to the site they had acquired at the junction of James Street and John Street, giving it the name of Providence Chapel. By 1859 the brethren found that their new James Street premises had become too small, so they took the brave step of acquiring one of the finest sites in the new Victoria Park Company's estate, at the corner of West Park and Victoria Avenue, where in 1862 they opened their present magnificent church. The Providence Chapel was sold, apparently to trustees of the newly-formed Harrogate Mechanics Institute, one of whose greatest supporters was Richard Ellis. Renamed the Victoria Hall, the former St John's Chapel became a centre of the education of working men, until the last quarter of the 19th century when it was demolished and replaced by a bank.

The accompanying picture shows the Victoria Hall in about 1880, photographed from the spot where today may be found the main entrance to Hooper's store. In the background rises the bulk of the Prospect Hotel – now the Imperial. The site of the re-erected Chapel of St John is now occupied by Beattie's Toy Shop, the filthy stone façade of which may fool people into thinking that it once formed part of the ancient St John's Chapel.

Beluah Street premises, *c.1910*, contained many varied businesses, including no less than five boot dealers. At number 23, Edward Pearson had his photographer's studio, next to which were the premises of the Beulah Commercial temperance hotel.

Station Square, during the spacious days of Edward VII.

A Parliament Street float, *c*.1912, passes premises which in 1999 were occupied by Yate's Wine Lodge and the Hogshead.

Parliament Street's wide pavements, captured in this view of *c*.1905.

Montpellier Stray shelter

Following an article about the two Victorian shelters in the grounds of the former Royal Bath Hospital, which have been re-erected in Valley Gardens and St Mary's Walk, the author was pleased to receive the fine postcard reproduced here. Certain areas of Harrogate were traditional sites for carriage stands, such as Park Parade, Montpellier Hill and St Mary's Walk, which served the needs of visitors to High and Low Harrogate. The so-called 'shelters' were never intended for public use, but were for the cabmen, being a little sanctuary for rest, protection from inclement weather, and a place to brew a pot of tea and get warm.

As the carriage trade declined, some of the shelters were converted into public shelters, such as the one opposite the Hospitality Inn on West Park, which may account for the fact that it still has a ventilator on the roof despite being open to the weather. In this postcard, the Montpellier Hill shelter may be seen, more or less at the spot where today may be found the zebra crossing. This shelter was moved across to St Mary's Walk, to provide a shelter for the taxi drivers, when they had a stand here, being demolished in the 1970s.

The erection of the hospital shelter at this location is therefore most appropriate, coming as it did from the Civic Society. At far left may be seen the premises of the Ackrill Press, who had recently occupied the building vacated by the Yorkshire Home for Incurables. On the horizon, may be seen from right to left the Prospect Hotel, Prospect Crescent, and the gable of the Café Imperial – today Betty's. Missing from this view of c.1905 is the tower of St Peter's Church, for it was not built until 1926. [Supplied by Mrs S. Sharan]

Valley Gardens Bandstand

Crowds listening to the musicians in Valley Gardens, one fine afternoon in about 1908. The bandstand was placed on the same site as the present building, but, being a completely circular structure, the exact point from which photographs were taken is often hard to identify with precision. In this case, the inclusion of a pavement well-head, provides the clue, and the picture can only have been photographed from Bogs Field, looking towards the north-east. The hedge – long since replaced with flowerbeds, whose sweet peas are a particular delight in summer – divided the Valley Gardens proper, owned by the Council, from the Bogs Field Circle, part of the Stray. This is no mere academic point, since any proposals to restrict access to the Stray part of Valley Gardens will invariably fall foul of the Stray Acts. Reports of anti-social behaviour, especially late at night, produce calls to close the Valley Gardens after sunset.

In York, the Museum Gardens retain their stout Victorian railings, and every evening, at dusk, the gates are locked, thus ensuring the security of the interior. The very size, irregular shape, and wartime removal of the Victorian railings, renders this solution impracticable in Harrogate. But the Stray Acts, which guarantee public access, are an even greater impediment to such nocturnal closure. Given the reported success of the CCT cameras in reducing crime and anti-social behaviour in central Harrogate, it may be possible to extend their use to Valley Gardens. The author recommends trying to re-educate any louts caught under this system, by sending them on a foreign holiday – preferably to Singapore. [Supplied by Mr G. Fowler]

Church House

Mrs E. Matthews' *History of Church House, Harrogate* is a carefully researched, well written and, above all, interesting account of that most useful social amenity in central Harrogate, Church House. In an eight-page booklet, Mrs Matthews relates the origins and development of the institution which today is housed at 19 Victoria Avenue, but which was founded in 1886 with rooms in Raglan Street and Princess Square. The ministers of Christ Church, St Mary's, St Peter's and St John's helped to establish the rules of the Institute, which were to unite the church people of Harrogate and its neighbourhood in strengthening and forwarding the work of the Church and to extend religious and general knowledge consistent with the principles of the Church of England. The Institute opened with 100 members, but subsequent growth caused the Institutes council to acquire a site in St Peter's Place – now Cambridge Road – between Cambridge Crescent and what is now the Post Office.

The new building was erected on one of the very last empty lots in central Harrogate, part of the old Carter estate, and was in a handsome gothic design. With its library, reading room, and lecture room for 250 people, the new Church House was a valuable addition to the town's amenities. Opened by the Lord Bishop of Ripon on 15 February 1889, the Church Institute operated successfully from the site until 1963, when it was sold, the current building at 19 Victoria Avenue being then acquired. The new building, Roxburghe House, had been home to one of Harrogate's most famous Spa doctors, Dr Gerald Veale, pro-chancellor of Leeds University. The accompanying photograph shows the site of the old Church House in Cambridge Road, shortly after its demolition in 1966.

Stray Encroachments

A considerable volume could be written about the various attempts by certain people to encroach upon the Harrogate Stray, usually with the best wills in the world, and of the equally sincere battles which blew up in attempts to defeat them. Here, however, a paragraph must suffice, and the author admits to a particular dislike of cyclists riding on public pavements. This is not to deny that the majority of cyclists are admirable people, who as children gave their pocket money to the poor, and as adults became card-carrying members of the RSPCA. But, the Stray has survived precisely because previous generations of townspeople have successfully resisted well-meaning proposals to convert bits of it into permanent parks, conference centres, exhibitions halls, sports arenas, heliports, boating lakes, hullah-hoop enclosures, skate-boarding rinks, or for any other usage devoted to whatever craze was the flavour of the month.

It may be recalled that the first efforts to improve traffic flow at Granby Corner came unstuck precisely because the Stray Acts prevent any alteration to the Stray planned to do anything other than enhance the Stray. They do not permit alterations on the ground of general road safety, vehicular traffic flow, or lobbying by users of particular kinds of vehicle. By no stretch of the imagination can the construction of tarred strips, parallel to selected Stray footpaths, be classed as an enhancement of the Stray. Such construction would be infinitely less attractive than the flower beds which were constructed on West Park Stray in 1932-33, in breach of the Stray Acts. The accompanying photograph shows the illicit beds being removed in 1934, after the ratepayers had removed most of the Council which had allowed their construction.

King's Road

Walker Road would be a better title for this article, for that was indeed its name when this photograph was taken in about 1908. To gain an idea of where the photographer must have stood in taking this view, one must stand at the junction of De Ferrieres Avenue with King's Road, and look north. Today the premises at far right are occupied by Threshers, and the shop at the corner of Skipton Street is now a hairdresser's. Most of these buildings are still in place, although the mock-Tudor structure in the distance was demolished – after a fire – and has been replaced with the Hill and Amos premises. King's Road, at least its northern section, does not feature on many postcard views.

Originally known as Baker Lane, the change to Walker Road took place later in the 19th century, lasting until 1910, when it was renamed King's Road to commemorate the accession of George V. Although the majority of building in King's Road dates from the 1880s and 1890s, the route is one of the oldest in Harrogate, being part of the ancient route between Low Harrogate and old Bilton. Evidence for this comes from the names and bounds of the fields on the north-east side, which can be traced back at least until the 14th century, many of which formed part of the medieval 'Crookisnab'. However, when the author visits King's Road today, he is more interested in the splendid shops, one of which sells his favourite pickled herrings.

Pier Head or Prospect Terrace

The neglect and closure of the Pier Head public lavatories was one of the least excusable facts of life in late 20th-century Harrogate. Some readers may recall that the public lavatories – so convenient both for visitors arriving at the coach stops in St Mary's Walk, as well as for the town centre – and the terrace formed on the roof, were built a hundred years ago, thanks to the 1893 Act of Parliament which permitted such a structure to be built on Stray land. The Act empowered Harrogate Corporation to build lavatories on the Stray, subject to the provision that if such lavatories were within 75 yards of an existing enclosure – i.e. building – then they must be placed under the ground.

Harrogate Corporation overcame this constructional difficulty, when the lavatories and terrace were built in 1896-97, by means of removing soil from the top of Montpellier Hill, constructing their building, and then covering it with soil removed for the excavation. The roof was provided with a paved terrace and banks of seating, and fitted with ornamental lamps and railings. Visitors soon found Pier Head to be a pleasant place to sit and enjoy the views of Low Harrogate, as well as the antics of the pierrots and street musicians, who established their pitches here shortly after 1898. Even the best constructed buildings fall into decay if they are not properly maintained, and decades of neglect throughout the later 20th century told their tale by c.1990. At the time of writing the lavatories are now boarded up, and the once pleasant roof terrace defaced with grim, crumbling tar, overgrown shrubs which obliterate the view over Low Harrogate, and a litter of ugly miscellaneous street furniture.

An Edwardian high summer on Harlow Hill, 1907

Here is a splendid photograph of Harlow Moor and its bandstand, typical of such structures erected by the Council on Harlow Moor, Bogs Field – which can also be seen in this picture – Crescent Gardens and the Spa Rooms Gardens. Today only the Bogs Field bandstand is on its original site, after having been replaced in 1933 with a new structure. The Spa Rooms bandstand was sold to Ripon when the Kursaal was built in 1903. In this photograph, taken in 1907, an audience has assembled to watch a performance by Tom Coleman and his Pierrots. Tom Coleman was one of Harrogate's best-loved entertainers, who performed from a number of pitches throughout the town, which he rented from the Corporation, some of which included Bogs Field, Pier Head, Crescent Gardens and lower Montpellier Parade. He also ran a music business from premises in the old Lowther Arcade.

The Council also employed musicians, purely for the purpose of providing visitors and residents with an agreeable amenity. The idea that they should produce a profit came in only after World War One. In those long-ago Edwardian summers, the belief persisted that it was as reasonable to spend money on street music as it was on ornamental gardens, promenades and the Stray. [Supplied by Mr D. Wilcockson]

Almsford Bank

In about 1905, the principal means of transportation between Pannal and Harrogate was by railway, and so the horse-drawn carts and the pair of cyclists shown in this view, may well have been typical of traffic conditions on Almsford Bank in the days before the motor car. Much of this road had been improved after the Act of 1751, 'For repairing the roads from the Town of Leeds, through Harewood, to the south west corner of the Inclosures i.e. the Stray of Harrogate…', the work being supervised by Blind Jack the famous Yorkshire road maker. The point at which the road crossed the little River Crimple had long been considered inadequate, and, in 1833, the Turnpike Trustees were prosecuted at Pontefract Sessions for failing to keep 'Aumphrey Bank' in a state of repair. It was noted that the bridge had not room for two carriages to pass at the same time.

'Aumphrey' or Humphrey Bank was improved shortly before World War One, when Harrogate's own W. H. Baxter, inventor of the 'Knapping process' of road construction, paid for improvements at Crimple Bridge.

A favourite story from this locality dates from the time of the highwaymen, who robbed the coaches of the wealthy visitors as they rolled in and out of Harrogate during the Spa season. Before Beech Grove was built, a farm stood on the edge of the Stray, known as Foster's Farm – but let William Grange tell the tale: 'Foster lived in a large whitewashed house, not far from the side of what is now Beech Grove. This house was a favourite with the humbler sort of lodgers. Seats were placed under the trees, and here they used to congregate – the men with long church wardens (i.e. long clay pipes) and the women with handkerchiefs over their heads gazing at the wide expanse of the Stray, and field and wood. This Foster was a big-boned fellow, noted for immense strength and energy. The house was very lonely in winter, and during his absence one day a celebrated highwayman named Nevison entered, terrified the inmates, and stole a blunderbuss. Foster soon afterwards arrived, tracked the thief through the snow, overtook him on Humphrey Bank, wrestled with him, and secured both thief and gun.'

The horror of 1914

There is a dreadful poignancy about this photograph, taken in the high summer of 1914, as it shows the Harrogate Pals Company and 5th West Yorkshire Volunteers marching up Station Parade, shortly after the outbreak of World War One. Many of these young men never saw Harrogate again, their names being inscribed on the war memorial, built in 1923 in Prospect Square. In the background may be seen the cottages which had been built in the 1870s by the railway company, to house their employees. These cottages were demolished in the late 1930s, when the site was acquired by the bus company for the Harrogate bus station, which from c.1938 to 1991 provided the town with a splendidly convenient and well-designed bus station, the envy of less fortunate communities such as York.

Following the ruling of the late cabinet minister – the unspeakable Nicholas the-market-will-decide Ridley, who was responsible for the privatisation of the National Bus Company – Harrogate's bus station was sold to a property development company, who promptly demolished it. This was bad enough, but at least it was not the fault of Harrogate Council, who were powerless to prevent the calamity. But today, we in Harrogate should be expressing our concern over a matter about which our Council most certainly does have control – look closely at this photograph of 1914, and you will see that Station Parade was, at one time, planted with trees. Indeed, the Victoria Park Company, who developed Station Parade as well as Victoria Avenue, intended that both streets should be lined with trees, as indeed they were, until quite recently. At the time of writing, only one dying tree remains on Station Parade between One Arch and the Railway Station. Why are our town centre trees seldom replaced? What has happened in King's Road is set to recur in Station Parade, and this is a scandal.

A Majestic mystery

Although postcard views of the exterior of the Hotel Majestic are quite common, the interior has seldom been featured on a postcard. This view is therefore, an unusual one, featuring as it does the great Winter Garden, built with the rest of the Majestic in 1900. Winter Gardens became fashionable in the 19th century, when such famous examples as Decimus Burton's Royal Palm House, at Kew, Paxton's Conservatory at Chatsworth, or Charles Fowler's Syon House Conservatory, revealed the potential of iron and glass as building materials. Early examples of adding Winter Gardens to Harrogate Hotels include the Queen, in High Harrogate, and the Cairn Hydro, which still stands at the main Ripon Road entrance.

It was therefore not surprising that the two great hotels built in Harrogate at the opening of the 20th century – the Grand and the Majestic – both included a Winter Garden. Regrettably, both Winter Gardens have also been demolished. The loss of the Majestic Winter Garden is particularly unfortunate, as it provided the Ripon Road façade of the great hotel with an impressive architectural feature. It went in about 1972, just before the fashion for conservatories revived. What a magnificent attraction it would be today, especially for use as a banqueting hall and exhibition area. Look closely at the picture, and a statue will be revealed. This is the mysterious 'Wept of Wishton-Wish', a white marble statue of a female in semi-warlike costume, with a serene expression on her face. Extensive research has failed to identify the meaning of this cryptic inscription, and the statue certainly had nothing of weeping about it. It was undamaged during the bombing of 12 September 1940, but, when the conservatory was demolished over 30 years later, the statue was apparently sold to 'a large estate in Devonshire'.

The great charity cricket match, 1908

Many of the sporting activities reported in the Harrogate press in the years before World War One, were dedicated to raising money for various local charities. In the summer of 1908, one of the most important of these contests was the great charity cricket match, planned by the Harrogate Cricket Club. The idea was to introduce something a little different into the game, and give Harrogate people something of the flavour of cricket at an international level. Accordingly, the organisers hit on the idea of mounting a truly international contest between an 'all-England XI', and the 'West Indies'. Representing the 'all-England XI' were the Harrogate tradesmen's team, shown in the accompanying photograph, complete with their uniform of top hats and broad

red braces. The members were, back row: R. Preston, scorer, A. Tattersdill, W. J. Lambert, I. J.Waller, S. C. Holliday, A. Hewson and G. Coates, umpire. Middle row: O. Verity, W. Howard (captain), E. Annakin. Front row: F. Thornton, T. Moon, J. W. Ward.

The 'West Indies' team – again all local men – somehow did not look the part of true West Indian players, until someone had the bright idea of applying boot polish to their faces, arms and hands. Thus it came to be that Harrogate, on Wednesday, 5 August 1908, was able to publicise the unusual event of a great charity cricket match All-England XI v the West Indies. The latter team consisted of back row: C. Leng, A. Brooke, A. Wilby, N. Ellis, T. Porter, R. Richardson (umpire). Middle row: F. V. Ward, W. Bury (captain),

W. Heald, W. Fawcett. Front row: F. Leyland, R. D. Snow, E. Sunley. The second accompanying photograph shows the 'West Indian' team, shortly before the game began. The *Harrogate Herald* reported that 'at one o'clock, a procession was formed in Station Square, and, headed by the Temperance Band, proceeded to the cricket field. The weather was not at all favourable, being cold, and slight showers added to the discomfiture. Notwithstanding the adverse climatic conditions, however, there was good attendance… the Temperance Band played during the afternoon, and an entertainment was given during the Tea Interval by Mr Tom Coleman's pierrots.' The charity for which the match had been planned, was the Harrogate Infirmary, and the £20 sum raised was substantial, by pre-war standards. Who won? The *Herald* reported the 'All England XI' scored 113 runs, and the 'West Indians' 101.

And if any reader doubts the truth of the above, it may all be found in the editions of the *Harrogate Advertiser* and the *Harrogate Herald* which followed 'the great Harrogate charity cricket match of 1908'.

Royal Baths Entrance

Even before the contractors had finished their work, the Royal Baths building was subjected to alteration. This photograph shows Crescent Gardens taken from the western ramp leading from Crescent Road up to the main doors. In the background, Crescent Gardens in about 1948, and at left, the elaborate canopy of glass and cast iron, which protected guests from rain and sun. The original entrance design by architects Baggalley and Bristowe, envisaged a pair of ramps, shielded by a colonnade, which connected the porte-cochère with each of the two projecting pavilions at the main frontage. There were no steps leading down to the pavement, as the architects had intended all arrivals and departures to be made via the two ramps.

However, shortly before the Royal Baths were opened by HRH the Duke of Cambridge, on 3 July 1897, the Wells and Baths Committee decided to alter the design of the entrance ramp without telling their architects. This caused a row, especially when the architects discovered that their carefully planned system for carriages had been wrecked by the narrowing of the ramps. However, the building had only been in use for a few months, when, at their meeting of 15 November 1897, the Council decided to cut through the porte-cochère, and build a flight of steps to connect with the footpath on Crescent Road. The work was undertaken swiftly, but it was then found that visitors arriving by carriage, who were set down on the pavement, risked getting wet when it was raining.

Accordingly, the Council had to go to the expense of erecting an iron and glass extension to the porte-cochère, which was in place by the summer of 1898. This canopy, which appears on the majority of postcard views of the Royal Baths, survived two World Wars, being demolished only in about 1950. Bill Baxter, or 'Mr Harrogate', as he was known, told the author that the canopy had to be taken down because delivery lorries kept knocking into it. They should have been sent the repair bill!

Hitler and the Market Hall Clock!

On 3 September 1939, the people of Harrogate listened to their radios broadcasting the announcement by Prime Minister Neville Chamberlain that Great Britain had declared war on Germany. The disturbance this event caused to the pleasant ritual of life in Harrogate, may, perhaps, be imagined only by those who lived through those turbulent times. The first sign of change arrived before the civil servants, the military personnel, the evacuees, or even the rationing, and it took the form of rumour. During the second week of September, there was talk that 14,000 Whitehall officials were removing to Harrogate, in the expectancy of mass bombing raids on London. Several Harrogate residents claimed to have heard an announcement on German radio, issued by Dr Goebbels' Ministry of Propaganda, that the British Government were sending many of their Air Ministry personnel to a little place called Harrogate.

At this time, Harrogate had just received a new Market Hall, which had been built to replace the old market burned down in January 1937. The new market incorporated the famous clock, presented to the town by the Baroness Burdett-Coutts, which had been displayed in a splendid Italian renaissance tower, erected at the junction of Cambridge Street and Station Square, where it could be seen to best advantage. Unfortunately, the design for the new market placed the clock in a stubby tower overlooking

Cambridge Street, thus ensuring that it was hidden from view to much of Station Square. The accompanying photograph, taken in c.1954, shows how the clock was obscured by the pavilion over the Station Square entrance. Be that as it may, the citizens of Harrogate, were pleased with their new market, and proud of their fine clock. But in far-away Berlin – it was later said – a sinister attack was being planned to demoralise Harrogate by spreading a rumour that the famous clock of the new market of the World's Greatest Spa was slow.

Twenty years later, the *Harrogate Advertiser* carried accounts of those of the town's citizens who reported hearing Lord Haw Haw broadcasting from Berlin that it was known that the Harrogate Market clock was a full two minutes fast. Lord Haw Haw, or William Joyce, had attended Fascist rallies in Harrogate before the war. It seems that several people actually claimed to have heard this broadcast. There is, somehow, something singularly delicious about the thought of Dr Goebbels" Ministry of Propaganda pondering on means to demoralise Harrogate, at the very moment when the Nazi war machine was advancing through Europe, and the whole of the World was sliding into the abyss of total war. The clock is still remembered fondly by many in Harrogate, and if anyone can arrange for its resurrection, there is little doubt that they would received the gratitude of the entire town.

St Robert's Church, Robert Street

Following an article about an 1898 request by St Robert's RC Church, made to Harrogate Corporation, to be supplied with a separate water supply to work the new organ, a reader kindly sent the author this hand-tinted postcard view of St Robert's Church, taken at the corner of Robert Street and Station Parade. Roman Catholicism appears to have revived very slowly in Harrogate, following the Reformation of the 16th century, and when the Curate of High Harrogate Church wrote to the Bishop of Chester in 1789, he referred to there being only '8 papists – farmers and day labourers' in Harrogate, along with a single family of Presbyterians.

During the first quarter of the 19th century, an attempt to open a place of worship for Roman Catholics was bitterly opposed by the Minister of Low Harrogate Church, who ranted against the building of a 'Popish mass-house'. It seems that Harrogate's Roman Catholic population began to increase after

the opening of the railways, and in 1861, Dr Render, described as Vicar and Capitular was hiring a room in the Crescent Hotel for services, at a charge of £12 per annum. When this proved unsatisfactory, a larger room in the Somerset Hotel – today, Yates's Wine Lodge – was hired, at an annual rent of £18, with the pastor lodging at 11 James Street, which also served as a Presbytery. By 1864 a special school and a Presbytery had been built in South Station Parade, and in June 1873, the new St Robert's Church was opened by Cardinal Manning.

Further enlargements occurred, of which the most useful was possibly the school, which is not visible on the accompanying postcard. Following the opening of a new school in 1963 at Granby Park, the old Robert Street school was abandoned, and demolished in about 1969 to make way for a car park. This has opened up a gap in the Robert Street frontage, which really does need to be filled.

When Oxford Street was Chapel Street

When Oxford Street took its present name in 1908, having previously been called Chapel Street, it contained a variety of residential, as well as commercial buildings, many of which have been recently destroyed. It seems that the old footway between Low Harrogate's Sulphur Well and High Harrogate's Chapel of St John, crossed the farming fields of central Harrogate more or less following the modern route followed by the Ginnel, Oxford Street, One-arch, Park View, Kingsway, and Walkers Passage. Much of this land was purchased in 1810 by James Franklin, who paid Sir John Ingilby the sum of £9,000 for what is now the whole of central Harrogate between the Hotel Majestic and York Place – surely the most astute single purchase in the entire history of Harrogate.

Franklin subsequently leased or sold much of his land to individual developers, including members of the Simpson family, who by about 1820 had established themselves as hard-working builders.

Today, the name of Simpson is forever associated with the building of the Duchy Estate, between about 1895 and 1915, but that Simpson – David – was only one of a long line of distinguished Simpsons, and some of their earliest work was done around the little settlement of cottages and workshops which sprang up at what is now the junction of Oxford Street and Cambridge Place, including the old Ship Inn. This photograph of about 1908 shows at right part of the garden of Belle Vue, home of the famous Captain Thomas Thrush, whose public pronouncements on the incompatibility of Christianity and war caused a national sensation in 1825. It was destroyed by Marks & Spencer in 1969, who more recently have occupied the conveniently flattened site of Lowther Arcade, the Georgian cottages, and the old Ship Inn. At far left may be seen the manse of Wesley Chapel, which some Harrogate citizens may remember as the home of Schofield's store.

Cornell Studios

At the time of writing, this part of Harrogate is occupied by the Victoria Centre, built in 1992 when the market building was reconstructed. The group of buildings which filled about two-thirds of the plot of land between Cambridge Street and Queen Victoria's Jubilee Monument, were unworthy of the importance of their central location – with the possible exception of Goodrick's Chambers which faced Cambridge Street. In 1953, Harrogate Council implemented long-standing proposals to enhance Station Square, demolishing many of the commercial premises, and constructing pleasant gardens and an underground suite of lavatories. Premises demolished included Howden's – originally Greenwood's – Garage, Hodgson's barbers, Holroyd's dry cleaners, and – between these last two – Petty's Wedding Studio. The business had been originally established in 1906, and specialised in wedding photography. The property between Goodrick's Chambers and Hodgson's barbers shop may at one time have been the home of Harrogate's stationmaster.

The old Winter Gardens and Peat Baths

At right, the peat baths, partly demolished in 1954, had originally been built as a pump room for the wells on the estate, being erected in 1874 by George Dawson, then owner of the Crown Hotel estate. The picture also shows the manner in which the gardens were planted, the little island beds of which encouraged visitors to walk, by means of incorporating changing vistas and surprise views. When the Royal Baths were built in 1897, the inspiration for so many designs in English spa architecture had a German origin – like the Prussian-spiked lampposts, various spa treatments such as the Nauheim Bath, or the Kursaal. The shape of the finials atop the Winter Garden came from the pretty little Fortuna Portal in Potsdam, designed in 1701 by the Dutch architect de Bodt, who also worked on Wentworth Woodhouse near Rotherham.

The opening of the Chapel of Harrogate Ladies' College

On 29 September 1923, Harrogate's most prestigious school for girls celebrated the opening of its new chapel with a service of dedication by the Right Revd the Lord Bishop of Ripon. Harrogate Ladies College, founded by Mr G. M. Savery, had its first home at Dirlton Lodge on Ripon Road, before moving into the Oval, and then onto its present site in Clarence Drive. The college paid particular attention to the observance of religion, Sunday services being held in the main assembly hall. For several years before World War One, the school governors had expressed the wish to build a separate chapel, and in 1917, a committee was established for the purpose of achieving this objective. Two years later, the college purchased the materials of old St Mary's Church, on St Mary's Avenue. This sacred building had been erected in 1825 to serve Low Harrogate's growing population. Designed by the architect of the Royal Bath Hospital, Samuel Chapman, and consecrated in 1825, St Mary's Church was in the Early English style of architecture, with a great plain tower at its west front. By the turn of the century, the structure had become unsafe, and the decision was taken to build a new church – the present St Mary's on Harlow Terrace, which was consecrated on Ascension Day 1916. For a while, thought was given to possibly constructing the new chapel from – of all things – brown asbestos, but fortunately, this idea was dropped in favour of purchasing the fabric of the redundant St Mary's Church. This was wise, since the old church had been built of high quality material, whose subsequent undermining had been caused by the marshy nature of its site.

Harrogate Ladies' College prepared the foundations of their new chapel with more care, with work proceeding as soon as the war ended, and by 24 February 1923, the foundation stone was laid by the Minister of Education, the Right Honourable Edward Wood, MP in the company of Mayor of Harrogate, David Simpson. Externally, the walls of the new chapel were built from the stone of the walls of old St Mary's. Some changes were introduced, however. Instead of repeating the old tall, Early English lancet windows, the new chapel added a Clere Storey, with two lights, instead of three. The great, massive tower, was not reconstructed, being replaced by a large perpendicular gothic window, flanked by castellated octagonal towers. Internally, the chapel is very pleasing, with several features from the old St Mary's Church, including roof timbers and the chancel arch. Above this, the wheel window incorporates a fragment of glass from Ypres Cathedral, destroyed in World War One. Today, the chapel of Harrogate Ladies College continues to play a central role in the life of this important, internationally celebrated Harrogate institution. This role is not only a religious one, but also musical, as the College has long prided itself on its outstanding musical achievements. The organ, by Abbott and Smith, of Leeds, was designed partly with the help of the organist of St Peter's Church, Mr C. L. Naylor, being first played on Armistice Sunday, 1923.

Here is a generous view of Station Square, taken from the junction with Station Bridge. The photographer must have stood at the upper window of chemists Handford & Dawson to obtain this view, which contains much of interest. At left, the North Eastern Railway's Station Hotel, with its two splendid canopies of decorative iron and glass. These canopies were erected exactly one hundred years ago, for the purpose of ensuring that the hotel's customers could, on wet days, walk from their carriages to the hotel entrance, without getting wet. They were destroyed in the early 1950s, when appreciation of Victorian design was at a low point. A thousand pities, as they were a strong enhancement to whole square. At the centre of the picture may be seen the Jubilee Monument of 1887, which still had its elaborate gothic iron railings, another attractive piece of Victorian iron work, the removal of which in World War Two's metal salvage drive was a further loss. In the distant background, the tower of the old Market may be seen, with the market clock clearly visible. At the far right may be seen the hedge which bounded the yard of the railway station, and the footpath which leads up across station bridge. To return to the subject of canopies, many of the town's citizens will regret that so much of the town's iron work has been lost. At one time the whole eastern side of Commercial Street was fitted with glazed canopies, which were a really useful feature, as well as being decorative. Parliament Street, too, had far more than the few examples which remain. [Supplied by Mrs K. Bulmer]

Beulah Street

Beulah Street in about 1908. A protruding sign, at left advertises the Temperance Hotel, which occupied the building now used by a charity shop, but built originally for the Methodists as a chapel. The terrace of building at right was but a few years old when this picture was captured, and shows the characteristic Victorian bay windows at first-floor level; sadly, several of these bay windows have been removed, thus spoiling the balance of the building. Note, too, the colourful awnings, which protected pedestrians from sun as well as rain. Today, the awnings have gone, and Beulah Street has been pedestrianised, thanks in part to the co-operation of the traders who have created a pleasant shopping environment for the public. It is suggested that huge strides could be made if similar 'street associations' could be organised for such areas as Cheltenham Crescent and Parade, James Street, Parliament Street, and that neglected jewel, High Harrogate.

King Edward memorial

In the early years of the 20th century the increasing traffic on the old Walker Road in Harrogate was causing enough problems for the matter to be investigated by W. Baxter of Knapping Mount, inventor of the Knapping process of road surfacing. Baxter's answer was to pay for the widening and resurfacing of the road, which was to be renamed King's Road. The northern boundary was extended, taking in a magnificent line of trees which had formed an edge to the Spa Rooms garden. A fine new pavement was put down and ornamental seats and lampposts provided. Mr Baxter also paid for a new boundary for the gardens, consisting of a superb set of ornamental railings with gates leading in from King's Road. The whole works, completed in the summer of 1911, was dedicated to the memory of the late King Edward VII. At the time of writing, the King's Road promenade is an arid waste.

Valley Gardens, c.1880

Thanks to modern developments in the production of hardy winter flowering plants, and its wide range of trees and shrubs, Valley Gardens presents a colourful appearance to the visitor throughout the year. However, when the accompanying photograph was taken back in *c.*1880, there were few trees and shrubs, and certainly not a hint of bedding plants, even at summer's height. At this time, Valley Gardens comprised a footpath between the Sulphur Well and the so-called Bogs Field, a detached area of Stray, rich in mineral wells. The footpath ran along both sides of the stream, the south-eastern half of which was lost when the Valley Drive boundary was planted with trees. This photograph was taken from the Valley Drive section of the footpath, looking across Bogs Field. At top centre background may be seen the buildings of the first Royal Bath Hospital, of *c.*1824, which were mostly cleared away for the rebuilding of 1888.

Below this, runs the stone boundary wall which still stands, dividing the grounds of the former hospital from Valley Gardens proper. The Old Magnesia Well Pump Room of 1858, which still stands in the little Bog Garden, may also be seen, with its steeply pitched roof and gothic door. Just beneath this, at the centre of Bogs Field, is one of the few 18th-century well housings which survived into the middle of the 19th century. All around, the grass has been worn away by the numbers of visitors who frequented this place. The man appears to be standing on a site which today overlooks the New Magnesia Well Café, and the fall of the path denotes the point at which the stream from Valley Drive today passes behind the Magnesia Well Café. Although the Improvement Commissioners had planted a few shrubs and trees in the 1850s, little was done to improve the area until Queen Victoria's Golden Jubilee of 1887, when the Council announced a competition to properly plan the area.

Sun protection 1902 style!

On this fine summer's day of *c*.1902, sensible ladies protected their delicate skins from the coarsening effects of the sun, by means of a parasol, and this splendidly clear photograph contains at least three examples. At left, below the cabmen's shelter on Cornwall Road, a pair of baby-carriages may be seen, whose nursemaids, appear to be in close conversation. At right, a stout lady sits on one of the Stray seats, possibly reading. The recently constructed St Mary's Walk crosses the Stray from left to right, and its newly-planted saplings are well protected from vandals by means of iron palisades. The shadows indicate that it is mid-afternoon, and, at least outwardly, all is at peace. A decade later, this would change, as the motor car became part of public life, and World War One signalled the end of the old order. One of the greatest changes to occur in the coming decades, would be with the management of the Stray.

When this photograph was taken, the Corporation had been in control of the grass, or herbage, for a mere nine years, having acquired powers of control and management from the former Stray Gate Owners by the 1893 Act. The so-called Gate Owners had been empowered to depasture cattle on the Stray, according to the number of imaginary gates they held, each gate enabling a specified number of cattle to be depastured. However, when the Corporation took over in 1893, rights of pasturage passed to Harrogate Council. *Advertiser* readers have written with memories of cows on the Stray, a practice which appears to have lasted until the 1930s. This is by way of explanation. Photographs of Harrogate Stray, before the 1930s, invariably show that the grass was allowed to grow to a much greater length than is the current case. In this photograph, the boy at lower left appears to be sitting in quite long grass, which would have been grazed by cattle. Today, of course, the grass is allowed to grow to enable spring bulbs to die back.

Street Party, c.1919

The commemoration of the ending of World War One may have caused some readers to rummage through their family papers, in search of interesting items from that time. Because of the very personal and often poignant nature of such material, it may occasionally be found to contain items of a rare or unusual nature. An *Advertiser* reader has been kind enough to lend this postcard which may be only part of a wider series produced in that short-lived but euphoric atmosphere that marked the end of Word War One.

The picture shows a street party, with maypole dancing and other festivities, photographed during the summer of 1919 at the junction of Nidd Vale Road and Strawberry Dale. The maypole partly obscures the wall at the end of Nidd Vale Terrace, which is covered with a splendid display of advertising posters for the Empire Music Hall, BSA Bicycles, and Keating's Pills. Beyond may be seen the shunting yard of the railway goods station in Bower Road, and the houses in Dragon Road. The poignancy of this picture is that it appears to have been taken in the summer of 1919 towards the end of the terrible influenza epidemic, and that this epidemic, together with the preceding World War of 1914-1918, would have affected every single person shown in this photograph. Copies of the *Harrogate Advertiser* and *Harrogate Herald* for this period contain references to street parties and communal celebrations, but the subject has not been given the research it deserves.

Crown Place

Crown Place is seen here shortly before the removal of the Royal Pump Room's temporary annex, and its replacement in 1913 with the present handsome structure, opened by the Lord Mayor of London. Originally, Crown Place had consisted of a few ramshackled commercial properties backing on to the rear premises of the Crown Hotel. Thanks to Alderman George Dawson, one-time owner of the Crown, a number of improvements were effected after 1870, which continued after Dawson's untimely death in 1889. Much of the truly magnificent architecture of Crown Place dates from c.1884-86, and is the result of a deliberate policy of embellishing the most important location in Harrogate. The importance of Crown Place came from its proximity to the World's strongest known Sulphur Spring, which attracted

visitors from all over the world. It was the fashion for such visitors, after they had consumed the waters at the Royal Pump Room, to parade along Royal Parade, and to congregate in Crown Place as this fine c.1903 postcard shows.

After World War Two, Crown Place was allowed to decay, the Yorkshire stone flags being hidden beneath the same tarmacadam [which at the time of writing, still ruins Pier Head] and the space given up to lazy motorists to dump their vehicles across the public footpath. However, following the Councils admirable restoration of the Royal Pump Room in 1987, and its re-opening by HRH the Duke of Gloucester, Crown Place was itself restored, being re-paved with natural stone, and provided with bollards to discourage illicit car parking.

New College

College Street and College Road meet Otley Road near the crown of Harlow Hill, and there is something of a mystery about the origin of their names. There are possibly only two explanations: first, that because they were preceded by a footpath which formerly ran from Harlow Hill, via open fields and Green Lane, to Lead Hall Lane, home of New College, they record a destination; second, they record St George's College, which was a handsome building at the junction of Otley Road and Harlow Moor Road, demolished in 1976 to make way for the present Swinton Court. With reference to the former explanation, New College, pictured opposite, was founded originally as Turton Hall, at Gildersome, in 1850, but, by about 1895, it had so outgrown its premises that the headmaster, Reverend John Haslam, sought fresh accommodation.

In 1878, one of the Turton Hall pupils had been a 12-year-old boy, Joseph Taylor, who later became Joseph Turner Taylor, Town Clark of Harrogate from 1898 to 1935. It is interesting to speculate if some memory of his former pupil drove headmaster Haslam to think of Harrogate, when he was seeking new premises for the school. Whatever the cause, the Reverend John Haslam visited Harrogate, inspected a site in Lead Hall Lane, and decided that it would be an ideal spot for his school. Having purchased 34 acres, Revd Haslam built New College, and set about the running and promoting of his establishment, which boasted six resident masters, and six visiting masters or professors. New College could contain 100 boarders, and the terms ranged from between 40 to 60 guineas per annum for British pupils, 100 guineas for foreigners. According to its prospectus, Harrogate was selected as the most suitable locality, as "it is acknowledged to be the finest district in the United Kingdom for growing youths, to whom it gives a certain indefinable buoyancy of spirits to those fortunate enough to live within its influence."

Dr Haslam died in 1917, being succeeded by W. J. Haslam, who in turn retired in 1927, three years before New College was purchased by Ashville in a virtual amalgamation of the two schools. It was finally demolished in about November 1970 and redeveloped with a housing estate.

The old Harrogate Town Crier

Harrogate's citizens should feel a certain pang of irritation when town criers from such resorts as Whitby and Robin Hood's Bay, dressed in full 18th-century costume and calling "Oyez, oyez…" are imported to open new developments in the town. And before anybody chips in with the comment that Harrogate has never had a town crier of its own, let the author relate the story of John Hodgson. Historian William Grainge noted that in the early 19th century, the post of Harrogate Town Crier was occupied by one John Hodgson, who was a total abstainer, and who appointed himself to the role of town crier, to the ire of the Township Authorities. Hodgson placed himself within site of a public house, and after announcing news to the gathered crowd, would advise them 'to feed pigs, not publicans'.

Given the influence of the innkeepers at this time, it is hardly surprising to relate that John Hodgson was somehow removed – Grainge writes of him being starved out The authorities must have realised that the work of town crier needed to be regularised, so they appointed John Hodgson's son to the post. The Hodgsons may have been related to the Hodgsons who leased the old Promenade Inn later called Hodgson's, and now Hale's in the middle of the 19th century, which in turn may account for the favoured pitch of the Harrogate town crier being at the Old Sulphur Well opposite Hale's Bar. John Hodgson junior had, along with his bell, another novelty attraction in the form of his infant son, David. John's public cry was 'To be sold by hauction by little Divid Hodshon, a hempty bag with a cheese in it an hudder valuable hemplements' – Grainge's spelling is copied.

John Hodgson's trade proved so successful that a rival soon appeared in the form of Thomas Clapham, who also called himself town crier, entering into a fierce contest with the older practitioner. In the summer of 1847, the two men tried to eclipse each other in the rival art of cock-crowing, and a fight broke out, to the annoyance of the authorities, and the gratification of the public. This led to the justice room, and a ticking-off by the magistrates. Shortly after, Hodgson died, and Clapham was left to cry alone, being subsequently appointed to the role of Harrogate Town Crier. Perhaps our Council might think about reviving the post!

Bus station's early days

The association of Harrogate Railway Station with neighbouring facilities for coach and bus travel is assumed by many to date from the building of the bus station in 1938. In reality, the association is very much older and originates with the hiring of horse-drawn carriages from the station forecourt. By the time this photograph was taken (c.1918) horse-drawn carriages had largely been replaced by motorised vehicles. Charabanc trips to Studley Royal were especially popular with visitors who boarded this stately vehicle in Station Yard and which had the road almost to itself. As a further inducement to custom, the proprietor provided a portable phonograph to reproduce the latest popular music at picnic sites. Following the deregulation of bus services in 1986, Harrogate's bus station passed into the ownership of Parkdale Properties and the long and sorry saga of closure and decay began. Surely there is not a single person in Harrogate who would not welcome assurances that our old association of trains, buses and taxis will long continue to operate from a central and convenient position.

Passing of a great orchestra

Harrogate Symphony Orchestra, greatest rival of the Bournemouth Symphony Orchestra, was photographed here on the eve of the successful world tour of 1999, which carried the fame of Harrogate around the globe.

Well, actually, no!

Unlike Bournemouth, Harrogate abolished its municipal orchestra in 1930, ending the Victorian belief which regarded the provision of great music as being at one with the provision of parks, museums, libraries and art galleries.

This photograph really shows the municipal orchestra with its famous conductor Julian Clifford posing on the steps of the Kursaal promenade the day before its augmentation for the British provincial performance of Elgar's *Second Symphony*.

Julian Clifford the showman conductor, had taken over the orchestra in 1906, inviting the world's greatest artistes to appear on the Kursaal's stage Kreisler, Melba, Tetrazinni, Busoni, Paderewski and Elgar himself.

The promenade still exists behind the Royal Hall bar but the gardens have vanished beneath the ugly sheds of the Exhibition Halls.

Ward's, Albert Street

The building which once housed Ward's Funeral Equipages in Albert Street still stands, almost unaltered in its upper portion. But there have been one, two, three major re-constructions since this photograph was taken c.1912. This shows part of the Albert Street terrace which grew from H. E. Bown's Princes Square development of 1867. The archway, left, led through to the rear of the premises and was used by D. S. Ward's business which hired out the then new-fangled motorised hearses. It was Ward's proud boast that he "put away the quality of Harrogate". The business also sold Shell motor spirit and hired cars, a service which was especially popular with visitors to the town. After World War One the whole ground floor was rebuilt to form a garage, which was itself converted into a fire station. Finally, the fire station made way for the present commercial conversion in 1987, when a solicitors property service opened its doors.

Scenes from yesteryear – Harrogate House

At one time, Harrogate Corporation owned the entire block bounded by Parliament Street, Crescent Road, Montpellier Road and The Ginnel. Following the sale of the land at the corner of The Ginnel and Parliament Street, the cottage properties were demolished to make way for the present concrete and glass pile of Harrogate House. Although of no architectural or historical value, the properties were an interesting reminder of the time when modest lodging houses were built along the old turnpike road from Leeds to Ripon for the accommodation of those visitors who could not afford the more luxurious fare at the Crown or the George. The corner shop, in the days before the nationalisation of the country's electricity supply, was used to market local services. What of Harrogate House? Some may suggest that it should be demolished for the construction of a multi-storey car park which would serve the retail requirements of both Parliament Street and the Royal Baths estate, but others might prefer to see it refurbished.

New Exhibition Hall and offices – 1950s style

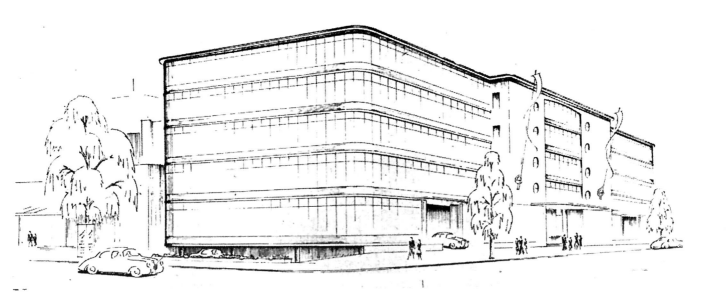

Public appreciation of Georgian and Victorian architecture was underdeveloped in 1954, so it is not surprising that when the *Advertiser* printed proposals for the rebuilding of the Spa Rooms site at the corner of King's and Ripon Roads, they depicted a design in the best 'modern' style. This had been submitted by Mr H. E. Taylor, and consisted of a new exhibition hall with basement car park and office facilities. There was at this time much talk of building something on this site which would reflect Harrogate's up-to-date image, and the Taylor scheme was certainly that, employing elements from the recent Festival of Britain style in London. At left may be seen the Royal Hall, and at right, King's Road. A further scheme in the 1960s to show how 'up-to-date' Harrogate could be, proposed a tower block with red and blue pre-cast concrete panels, and much glass.

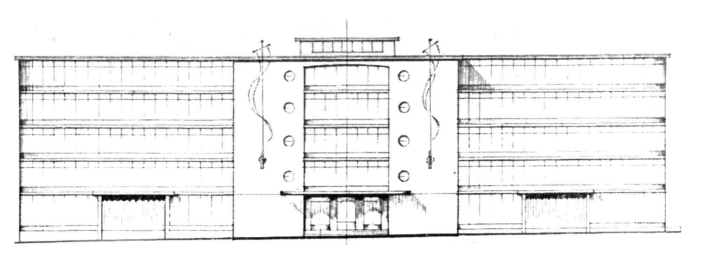

Valley Gardens water feature

The Valley Gardens have their origin in the footpath which connected the Sulphur Well with Bogs Field. In 1887, the year of Queen Victoria's golden jubilee, Harrogate's council began a series of improvements to the area which included the planting of trees and shrubs. The stream which drained water from Harlow Hill was incorporated into the gardens as a water feature, and a fountain was provided. Finally a solitary swan was obtained and, shortly after, the council debated whether they should not obtain a second swan to prevent the existing bird from becoming lonely. In the 1980s, a colony of ducks became well established, to the delight of the children.

Taylor's the Chemist

Taylor's the Chemist (pictured here shortly before 1914) receives a delivery of the famous Farrah's Harrogate Toffee. Taylor's had premises at 16 Beulah Street, 2 Cambridge Crescent and 54 Station Parade, and was an old, established Harrogate company. In the background can be seen one of the strangest buildings in Harrogate, the Theosophical Hall which was part of the Arcade of 1902. With its red brick and stone facings, this Dutch gable linked-up with the neighbouring Lowther Arcade and provided pedestrians with a useful covered link between Beulah Street, Cambridge Street and Oxford Street. In 1998, this latter structure was refurbished by Argos Sports Intersport.

James Street

But for the cars facing the wrong way, this picture of James Street looks as if it could have been taken yesterday. However, closer inspection reveals the street, which took its name from land speculator James Franklin, has changed a great deal since this scene was captured around 1946. The impressive premises of Marshall and Snelgrove, a great British institution for displaying and selling high fashion, is now the Hooper's department store. Further along, Maxwell Grayson's wine and spirit merchants on the junction with Cross James Street has been demolished and replaced by a concrete building selling bags and cases. The traffic island with its ornamental lamppost, which formed an important *point-de-vue* from Princes Square, has been swept away. Behind the scenes there have been changes too. The carriage trade has disappeared and no longer do the chauffeur-driven Rolls Royces and Bentleys deposit their owners into the solicitous care of such stalwarts as the doormen of Marshall and Snelgrove's or Standing's. And, I wonder, are there still any parents who warn their children: "Best behaviour, mind – we're going into James Street!"

Conservative Club

The shop at the corner of Cambridge Street and Beulah Street occupies part of the structure of *c.*1881 which had once been the home of the Harrogate Conservative Club and St James's Coffee House. Although the ground floor has been transformed by its conversion to retail premises, the upper levels are almost unchanged. Far left may be seen the separate entrance to the St James' Hall where a great novelty was presented to the public on 25 December 1908 – animated pictures. The round-arched window at left was demolished to make way for the Marks and Spencer store. At far right may be seen the main entrance to the former Conservative club with its characteristic tower and portico. It was from this balcony that Samson Fox addressed his supporters following his victorious County Council election campaign of 1901. Always a keen promoter of the preservation of British trade, he had previously given a rousing speech on the subject in St James' Hall in 1885. St James' Hall eventually became the St James' Cinema, which will be remembered by older Harrogate people.

Esplanade House

The two handsome properties on the Esplanade, known as Beech Lodge and Beech Villa, recently restored by a Yorkshire businessman, were typical of the exacting standard required of developers by the Duchy of Lancaster who oversaw the development of this area in the years following 1850. Older residents may recall a third mansion which, until the 1960s, stood across from Beech Lodge on the other side of St Mary's Walk. This was Esplanade House, family home of the Holroyd family, including the talented brothers Joseph and Thomas. The latter was a successful artist and photographer and travelled widely after being trained in London, Paris and Rome.

When in Canada, Thomas painted a celebrated series of portraits of Indians in the Mohawk settlement. His brother, Joseph, presented Harrogate with the famous picture by Herring of the Horse Fair, which is now one of the treasures of the Mercer Gallery. The studio at the rear of Esplanade House had an interesting connection with Queen Victoria – Harrogate's statue that is! On May 19, 1887, a 4.5 ton block of white Sicilian marble was delivered from the railway station and set up in the Esplanade House studio, where for five months the London sculptor Webber worked on it. The statue was a gift from Mayor Richard Ellis to mark the golden jubilee of Queen Victoria, which still graces Station Square. Esplanade House fared less well, being demolished to make way for a hideous tower block which, hopefully, will one day be replaced with something more in keeping with one of Harrogate's most interesting addresses.

Parliament Street

Following the death of Harrogate's celebrated Medical Officer of Health, Dr Titus Deville, his Parliament Street residence was purchased by a property developer for the erection of a shopping arcade (far left). Opened in 1897, the arcade boasted a gloriously exuberant gothic frontage which still remains Parliament Street's most striking piece of commercial architecture. The building was occupied by Charles Walker's furniture store following the closure of the arcade but in 1983 was restored to its original purpose, being named Westminster Arcade. The older properties (pictured right) were acquired by Buckley's department store (later, Busby's and today Debenham's) and demolished in the 1950s to provide room for an extension to the store.

The old Buckley's was a marvellously old-fashioned establishment by the standards of the author's childhood memories of *c.*1956. One feature stood out in particular. The store was criss-crossed with wires along which hurtled canisters containing moneys or receipts for goods purchased. The canisters were fired by means of a trigger and fairly zinged along to the intense enjoyment of at least one small boy. These delights were as nothing, however, to the sight of the nerve-centre for the flying transactions, which was a sort of cage, suspended from the ceiling, from which peered a solitary and cross-looking female. On enquiring who she was and why was she in the cage, the explanation was: "She's been a very wicked woman and is being punished by God!" This invariably shut the author up for at least ten minutes as he speculated on the nature of the wickedness!

Standing's

This picture features Edward Standing's café and grocery in Harrogate, which first opened its doors for business in 1882. On the corner of James Street and Station Square, it contained a basement smokeroom lined with oak panels, a ground-floor grocery, an oriental café on the first floor and a second-floor bakery. Much of the building's rich, decorative features were lost after World War One when the stained-glass panels were removed from the windows and modern signage introduced. Much to the regret of many regular customers, Standings closed in February 1982.

Wordsworth walk?

At the time of writing, the saplings pictured in this engraving, which flank the footpath between Prince of Wales Mansions and Tewit Well, have been growing for about 140 years, and, sadly, some are beginning to show signs of decay. Although a strong case can be made against turning the Stray's majestic broad acres into a series of small tree-lined enclosures, this line of trees must be an exception. This print of the Chestnut Walk was published in 1872 by the Rock company.

The Rock prints, which are not uncommon, were issued as steel engravings throughout the later 19th century, often in strip form. A few extra drawings seem to have been done, which were not issued with the main series, and this print is one such. It is taken from south Stray, looking due west, towards Leeds Road, and includes the eight stately mansions – all of which survive to this day – occupying sites as far as Otley Road. These mansions are a wonderful assemblage of high Victorian domestic residential architecture, whose historic significance was enhanced by the erection of Trinity Church which was built from 1877 to 1879 on the site in front of the three right-most mansions. The interiors of these great houses, with their quality of workmanship, are really stunning.

As for the trees, they were planted at the instigation of Richard Ellis and his fellow Improvement Commissioners, back in 1860, when it was felt necessary to provide visitors with pleasant tree-lined walks. This same path was used by the Wordsworths when they stayed in Harrogate in 1823. Mary, the poet's wife, in a letter of 20 July, refers to a stay at Hattersley's Hotel – today the Prince of Wales Mansions – and of William Wordsworth's eyes and face benefiting from the Waters. At the time of the Wordsworth's visit, the Tewit Well waters were used not only for drinking, but also for the bathing of tired eyes ! In view of all this, it might be nice to consider giving the Chestnut Walk an official name. The Stray already has a Milton Way and a Byron Walk, so how about Wordsworth Walk?

[]

The Master Builder's outing

One of the best aspects of having the privilege of sharing these photographic mementos of old Harrogate with readers, is that the author is often sent pictures that are wholly new to him. This photograph of Parliament Street is one such. Unfortunately, there is nothing on the photograph to identify its precise date or subject, but it appears to record one of the annual outings arranged by the Harrogate's master builders and their families, which were a regular feature of the town's social calendar in the last century. At this time, the master builders were a real power in Harrogate, having largely succeeded the innkeepers in their role of being the only class to rival the supremacy of the Spa's doctors. Men such as Richard Ellis, George Dawson, Charles Fortune, Isaac Pickard and the Chippendale family were notable examples of the master builder class, although by the late 1890s Alderman David Simpson had assumed the mantles once worn by the late Messrs Ellis and Dawson. The outings were elaborately staged affairs, which visited destinations as far as the Dukeries, where picnics were enjoyed. The lengthy processions often began in Parliament Street, where the master builders and their guests climbed aboard coaches. Weighed down with the mass of paraphernalia without which no Victorian picnic was complete, including several casks of ale provided by the Somerset Hotel, the procession then departed, to the accompaniment of blasts from the postilions horns. [Supplied by Miss Stacey]

Wartime St Wilfrid's

An uncommon view of St Wilfrid's Church, taken from the junction of Duchy Road and Kent Avenue, and published as part of a postcard, whose postage stamp is dated 1916. The point of interest is the

incomplete state of the north transept, which has subsequently been brought to its present perfection, with the porch, or north, entrance. It may be that the north front of St Wilfrid's was originally destined to receive a large traceried window, rather than the present characteristic porch, which may remind some of parts of Wells Cathedral.

St Wilfrid's, it may be recalled, had been opened in January 1908, with the dedication of the nave and baptistery. By June 1914, the nave, chancel and two chapels were ready for consecration by the Bishop of Ripon, and it was in this condition that this photograph was taken. The building of St Wilfrid's Church – designed by the great Temple Moore – received essential support from a Miss Trotter, who died in 1924, and it was she who left £32,000 for the completion of the structure. Her generosity is recorded in the initials on the stone Calvary at the north door: 'A.M.D.G. in Mem. E.S.T.' [Supplied by Mr C. Hopes]

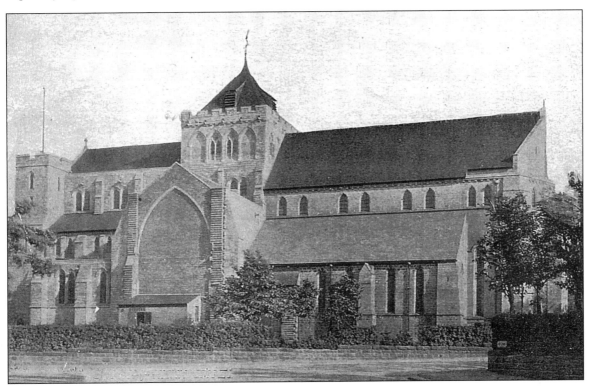

Wood's Grocery Emporium

If there is one retail activity of old Harrogate that should be revived today it is that of the town centre grocer. To have in James Street, an establishment such as Northallerton's Lewis & Cooper, would be a great thing. Today, many older Harrogate residents will recall Standing's, at its historic location on the corner of James Street and Station Square. Standing's, however, had been established in 1883, and for many years, there was only one significant grocery in what is now called central Harrogate – Wood's Grocer's Emporium. This photograph shows Wood's Grocer's Emporium in James Street some ten years before Standing's shop was built.

The business appears to have been established in October 1872, occupying part of the impressive new building erected in 1870 by Alderman George Dawson – premises which today are occupied by Ogden's. John Wood, who died at an advanced age in 1904 and who practised the honest old Yorkshire habit of looking people straight in the eye during conversation – and who in consequence refused to use the telephone – had back in the 1860s, spotted the business potential of central Harrogate.

Determining on a grocer's trade, he opened a shop in Alderman Dawson's recent development, which grew into one of Victorian Harrogate's most successful institutions. His staff included a hard-working lad called Greaves, who began working in Mallory's village store in Spofforth, who was spotted by Wood and invited to join his business, where he worked until it closed in 1933. It is believed that Greaves' son later became a grocer at Woodlands, and also sub-postmaster. Those were the times when a wise employer encouraged loyal staff to stay with the firm. Wood also employed a boy, whose principal task was to bring goods from a special store, on an upper floor at the back of the shop. Because the boy seldom stayed for long, John Wood refused to use personal names, calling him simply 'the boy'. The regular order was: "Boy! Step up and get me…" Consequently, the post was known as the 'step-up-and-get-me' job.

Back in Wood's prime, the James Street grocer's shop was flanked by Colonel Harrison's bank, which later became the Bradford Old Bank, moving across the road to the site of today's Barclays building. His other neighbour was the well-known 'Jewel John Jackson', a jeweller, who liked to walk up and down James Street, greeting the elegant lady visitors, and complementing them on their hands: "What a pretty little hand, what a fine little hand, why I've never seen such a pretty little hand. Why not bring it in to try my rings?" By contrast, John Wood stayed in his shop, supervising the delivery of orders, which came from miles around. In those days, it was common for carriages drawn by pairs, or sometimes four-in-a hand, to draw up outside the shop, the sound of their hooves kept to a minimum because of the wooden blocks with which James Street was surfaced.

Teas, coffees and spices were blended only on the premises, and the shop interior was always in a state of semi-darkness, as the huge James Street windows were blocked in by display panels, illumination being provided by spluttering gas globes. The hams, boiled on the premises, were a local speciality, some being supplied to the Czarina of Russia, who as Princess Alix, had visited Wood's shop during her holidays in Harrogate. John Wood also dealt, in another part of his shop, with old china, ivories and Japanese goods, being something of an authority of antiques.

One of his customers was Dr Titus Deville, Harrogate's formidable Medical Officer of Health, who lived in Parliament Street on the site of the Westminster Arcade, driving through the town, clad in his famous scarlet silk cloak, in a splendid carriage drawn by a team of white horses. Dr Deville manufactured home-made liquors purely for medicinal purposes and obtained many of his ingredients from Wood's Emporium.

At Christmas the *Harrogate Herald* carried a description of the town's shops:

'The emporium of Mr John Wood, family grocer and provision merchant, of James Street… is noted for the choice blends of teas, excellence of provisions, including fine Yorkshire hams, bacon, Stilton, Wensleydale, and Cheshire Cheeses, which cannot be surpassed. His splendid stock of fruits are of the finest quality, the crystallised fruits being a magnificent and varied sample. A grand selection of articles for Christmas presents include Japanese cabinets, and other artistic novelties; also Vienna placques and vases of great beauty, Dresden ware etc. Tom Smith's crackers are a marvel in variety and construction, and, like the pretty baskets of chocolate and artistic caskets of fancy goods, constitute an unrivalled assortment. Every department has been replenished with new goods to supply the Christmas trade, and extensive demands upon well-known establishment.'

As may be imagined, Christmas eve was an especially busy time, and John Wood's Grocer's Emporium stayed open until there were no more customers. One of the kindest purchases from Wood's shop, at Christmas 1898, was made by Alderman David Simpson, who provided the inmates – as they were termed – at the Union Workhouse with a little

Christmas cheer. According to the *Herald*: 'On Thursday, Alderman David Simpson and Mrs Simpson repeated the treat they gave to the whole of the inmates a year ago ...An excellent knife and fork tea was provided ...and a ...grand concert ... at the conclusion of the programme, Alderman and Mrs Simpson presented each man with a packet of tobacco and the women with a packet of tea and sugar...' The tobacco had been provided by Joah Baxter, a little further up James Street, but the provisions came from the premises of John Wood's Grocer's Emporium, James Street, Harrogate.

VC holders and St Peter's Schools

On Wednesday 12 May 1999, The Mayor of Harrogate, Councillor Ruth Timmis, unveiled a plaque in Station Square, to the memory of the town's Victoria Cross holders. Thanks chiefly to the efforts of Mr L. Swales of Harrogate, the prime promoter of the project, the town now has a permanent and visible reminder of the achievements of some remarkable men:

Donald S. Bell was born in Harrogate on 3 December 1890, and enlisted in November 1914, being subsequently commissioned by the Green Howards in June 1915. He won the Victoria Cross on 5 July 1916 at Horseshoe Trench, Somme, being killed in action on 19 July 1916.

Charles Hull was born in Harrogate on 24 July 1890, and served with the 21st Lancers, winning his Victoria Cross on the North West Frontier, India, on 5 September 1915. He died in Leeds in 1953.

The first photograph overleaf shows 2nd Lieutenant D. S. Bell, VC, as he appeared in the Ackrill annual for

1917, subsequently reprinted in the *Advertiser* article by Mr R. Brook CBE, on 25 February 1994.

The photograph below shows D. S. Bell in 1914 when he was a schoolteacher in Starbeck, standing, at top left, with his class. The girl at extreme right, second row from the back, is Rosa Steele, mother of the Mr Graham who kindly supplied the photograph. The school was, of course, Starbeck Council School, at which D. S. Bell was a master, a post he managed to combine with that of professional footballer with Bradford Park Avenue.

The last photograph is of Charles Hull, a former postman, who had been in the Army since 1908, and who not only received the Victoria Cross, but also the French Croix de Guerre. Both Donald Bell and Charles Hull had, as children, attended St Peter's School when it was located at its original site in Cambridge Road, later to be occupied by the Regal Cinema, and after, by MacDonalds.

[Information supplied by Mr D. Bell, Mr R. Brooke, CBE; Mr M. Graham, Mr G.L. Swales. Photographs supplied by Mr M. Graham.]

An uncommon view of Tewit Well, which includes not only the attendant's cottage, but also, at far right, a section of Tewit Well Road which was under construction – although this last feature is very faint. The Tewit Well is, of course, the oldest Spa in England, having been identified in 1571 by Mr William Slingsby, and although mineral waters had been used long before – the Roman Bath at Bath being perhaps the most famous example in Britain – Harrogate's Tewit Well was the first such water to be designated a Spa.

It fell into dereliction in 1971, after – coincidentally – 400 years of continual public use. It is not known if the source survives, as works on the south Stray carried out by the Water Company passed perilously close to the well head, and precautions were not taken to protect England's oldest Spa.

Back in 1841, when Harrogate's waters were highly valued, the Improvement Commissioners built the new Royal Pump Room in Crown place, and transferred the old Sulphur Well Temple up to the Tewit Well, where it was re-erected. However, in view of the exposed nature of the site, the Commissioners decided to wall in the temple- which hitherto had been open – and to build a cottage for the well attendant. Architect Isaac Thomas Shutt designed the building, and adopted a Tudor rustic design, rather in the manner of a cottage orné.

Meanwhile, behind the Tewit Well, the fringes of the Stray remained unbuilt, and it was not until builder Pickard started developing the area, in the 1890s, that houses began to appear. Pickard seems to have had a nice sense of humour, as he tentatively named one of his new roads 'Pickardilly', which was too much for the Council's planning committee to stomach, who changed it to the present Alderson Road, in honour of Baron Alderson, of the great Thackwray Well Case of 1837. In truth, Pickard did more for Harrogate than Baron Alderson, but that's another story. [Supplied by Mrs Pearson]

St Peter's Church

Here is an unusual postcard view of St Peter's Church, photographed from the junction of Cambridge Road and Cambridge Street, in about 1908, by the Frith company, who recorded much of England in a series of photographic surveys. The Victoria Park Company's plans had always envisaged a church on this site, and as the speculating builder Alderman George Dawson developed his two great crescents – Cambridge and Prospect – it became obvious that the intermediate site would require a building of some substance.

As central Harrogate grew, there was talk of forming a new parish from the larger one of Christ Church, which received valuable support in the form of a bequest of £3,000 from a resident. In 1868 it was possible to commission George Dawson's architect, J. H. Hirst, to prepare designs for a new church. The foundation stone of St Peter's was laid on 21 April 1870 by Canon James, Vicar of Christ Church, the funds only allowing for the building of the present chancel, and a temporary brick nave. The incomplete building was opened by the Rt Revd Bishop Ryan, Vicar of Bradford, on 7 September 1871. Does a photograph of this brick structure exist ? Following further building, the enlarged church was consecrated by the Bishop of Ripon, Dr Bickerstaff, on 3 October 1876. Hirst's original conception for the completed church seems to have included a spire, which indeed appears on some of the Victoria Park company's plans for the area.

It was never built, probably because it would have required a spire matching that of Salisbury Cathedral to counter-balance the weight of the two flanking Dawson crescents. In the event, a great square tower was completed, in 1926, which is today such an impressive part of Prospect Square – although it would be nice if some generous citizen would contribute towards its cleaning! This view shows the lowest stage of the tower, plus, at far left, the old St Peter's School before it removed to its Avenue Road location to make way for the Regal Cinema. Although they cannot really be seen in this view, St Peter's Church was flanked with superb ornamental gas lamps and railings, the loss of which is 1940 is greatly to be regretted. [Supplied by Mrs A. Smith]

Harrogate's royal connections

There is irony in the fact that whereas there are some British Spas which have adopted the Royal prefix, on the slight grounds of some brief visit by a reigning monarch, Harrogate, which has a direct and unbroken royal link for 900 years, has – at the time of writing – never sought to capitalise its association with the British monarchy.

The first direct link between the community which settled the lands between the Anglo-Norse hill of Harlow, and the River Nidd, appears to have been in *c.*1100, when King Henry I is believed to have laid out the Royal Forest that subsequently came to bear the name of the largest and most important neighbouring settlement, Knaresborough, a settlement, incidentally, which lay beyond the Forest's northern boundary, formed by the River Nidd.

Within the Royal Forest, there developed a number of special enclosures, known as chases, parks, or woodlands, which were set aside for such purposes as the Royal Stud (as at Haverah), timber (as at Oakdale), or the depasturing of pigs and other livestock (as at Fulwith, Harlow or Bilton). In 1173, King Henry II leased the Royal Forest to the Stutevilles, but by 1234, it was back in royal hands, being held by Richard, Earl of Cornwall, brother to King Henry III. After a series of further transferences and reversions, the Royal Forest passed into the hands of King Edward II's favourite, Piers Gaveston, Duke of Cornwall. Following the death of Edward II and the subsequent removal and murder of Gaveston, the Royal Forest, including Harrogate, was again granted to Thomas, Earl of Lancaster. However, in 1372, when John de Montfort, Duke of Brittany, was wavering in allegiance between France and England, it was considered politic to grant him the honour and earldom of Richmond, which was then held by the Duke of Lancaster – otherwise known as John of Gaunt, or Ghent. By way of compensation, the Duke of Lancaster was given the Castles and Honors of Knaresborough and Tickhill. Harrogate, the earliest surviving documentary evidence for which dates from 1332, was from 1372 part and parcel of the Duchy of Lancaster.

After the death of King Edward III in 1377, the new King, Richard II, caused the Duke of Lancaster's son, Henry Bolingbroke, to go into exile in France. On learning of the death of his father, the new Duke of Lancaster, the exiled Bolingbroke, sailed to England to reclaim his title. He landed on the Yorkshire coast at Ravenspur at some time between 28 June and 4 July 1399, and, with his retainers – some of whom would certainly have included Harrogate foresters – marched on Pickering and then Knaresborough castles, which he occupied. Henry Bolingbroke, went on to enjoy further military success, before deposing King Richard II at Flint Castle, and seizing the crown of England. At his coronation on 13 October, 1399, Henry Bolingbroke, Duke of Lancaster, merged the possessions of the Duchy with those of the Crown of England. From the time of King Henry IV, Harrogate not only retained Ducal ownership, but it also became a royal one in perpetuity.

The outright ownership by the Crown of land which now forms the modern borough of Harrogate, continued through the houses of Lancaster, York, Tudor, Stuart and Hanover, until the time of George III. During the period of the Commonwealth, under Oliver Cromwell and his son Richard, the interesting situation arose whereby moves to extinguish the Duchy of Lancaster faltered, largely because of the difficulty encountered by the new authorities in replacing the Duchy's excellent courts. However, parts of the Royal Forest were sold, and in 1651, Thomas Stockdale and three associates were granted a lease of the Forest, assuming the title of Joint Lords. The Forest was, throughout this period, referred to as 'part of the possessions of Charles Stuart', so in one respect, the royal linkage was maintained.

When Charles Stuart returned as King Charles II, in May 1660, royal estates and kingly rights were restored to him, including those of the Duchy of Lancaster, and with it, the Royal Forest of Knaresbrough. However, the Harrogate portion of the Royal Forest regained by Charles II was smaller than that inherited by his father, Charles I, for the art loving king had, in 1628, sold the Harrogate parks of Bilton and Haverah to the city of London, who in turn re-sold them to the same Thomas Stockdale who in 1651, would lease the rest of the Royal Forest.

Royal ownership of the forest's freehold continued until the time of George III and the great Award of 1778, which enclosed the forest, auctioned the land, and – most importantly – gave the Harrogate mineral wells into public ownership, including the surrounding 200 acres of land, which were to be forever open and unenclosed. The Duchy very wisely retained ownership of the freehold of the Harrogate Stray, the better to guarantee the integrity of the 200 acres, and the continuing right of the public to enjoy unrestricted access to the Harrogate Spa. Other parcels of land were awarded to the Duchy, including the so-called Duchy estates. As with any other long term property owner, the extent of the Duchy's holdings has – since 1778 – fluctuated. It is, however, a simple truth that since 1399, the crown of England has owned significant parts of Harrogate. The fact that this Duchy connection has been to the overwhelming and irrefutable advantage of Harrogate, is shown in the *Harrogate Great Chronicle*.

In 1838, Leamington Spa was granted authority to add 'Royal!' to its name. The move was taken at a time when the spa found itself in dire difficulties, caused by a bad enclosure act, uncontrolled building speculation, and knowledge that the spa business was decaying. Tunbridge Wells obtained royal status by permission of King Edward VII, on the flimsy grounds of his having once visited Tunbridge Wells in 1881.

Unlike the two English Spa towns of Royal Leamington Spa and Royal Tunbridge Wells, Harrogate can boast of royal connections going back to *c.*1100. it may be a characteristic of the blunt Yorkshire folk who developed the Harrogate Spa that they felt no compunction about adopting for their town the Royal prefix, despite Queen Victoria's permissions to adopt it for the Royal Pump Room, the Royal Bath Hospital and the Royal Baths. But at the very end of the twentieth century, voices were heard in support of re-designating the town 'Royal Harrogate Spa'. Certainly, no other resort in England had a greater right to call itself a Royal Spa. That much was beyond doubt.

Crimple Valley Railway Viaduct

The Crimple Valley Railway Viaduct is one of the most impressive monuments to 19th century constructional engineering in England. It was built as a part of the York and North Midland Railway Company's line between Harrogate and Church Fenton, which entered Harrogate by way of a short tunnel under Follifoot Rigg The tunnel, known as Prospect Tunnel, knew a brief fame in the 20th century as the place where Prime Minister Churchill's train was briefly bunkered during his visit of 1944.

It is well known that before the central railway station was opened in 1862, there were two railway stations in Harrogate, one of which was the Brunswick, opened in 1848, more or less next to Trinity Church at the comer of Leeds and Otley Roads. The other was opened at Starbeck in 1849, being part of the Leeds and Thirsk Railway. Although it is sometimes thought that the Brunswick Station was on the line from Leeds, and the Starbeck Station on the line from York, the exact opposite was true. This can be understood when it is realised that the 19th century system of railway lines around Harrogate was far more detailed than that which exists today, and that it was the result of competition between two rival companies.

When the Starbeck Station opened in 1849, it was linked with Bilton junction, which in turn ran out across the River Nidd on the Bilton Gorge Viaduct, leading to Ripon and Thirsk. At this time, there was no railway link with Knaresborough. Access to Knaresborough from Starbeck was made difficult by the depth of the Nidd Gorge, but eventually a link was built by the East and West Yorkshire Junction Railway, being opened on 1 October 1851. The Starbeck line also ran south, crossing Wetherby Road and Crimple Valley, before arriving at Pannal Station, and the rest of the line to Leeds.

The Brunswick Station was terminus to the line which ran across the site of the West End Park Estate, entering a tunnel more or less at the junction of Leeds Road and Langcliffe Avenue, before emerging to join the line which continued over the great Crimple Viaduct towering over the railway line from Pannal to Starbeck, before entering the Prospect tunnel and the line to Church Fenton via Wetherby and Tadcaster.

Amalgamation of the various railway companies occurred on 31 July 1854 to create the North Eastern Railway Company, thus making possible the construction of a loop line between the route from Crimple Valley High Viaduct, and Bilton Junction and Starbeck. The proposed loop line and central Harrogate Station was made possible only by the good will of the Duchy of Lancaster and the diplomacy and skill of Alderman Richard Ellis, who negotiated the tricky matter of a railway line crossing the sacred Stray. In exchange for the loss of Stray occasioned by the new cutting, Ellis obtained the site of the old Brunswick Station, which was added to the main

Stray as compensation. As a director of the newly-formed Victoria Park Company, Ellis was also in a powerful position to provide an ideal site between High and Low Harrogate for a central station, which was eventually built, and opened on 2 August 1862.

The great viaduct at Knaresborough, which provided a link between Knaresborough and Starbeck, and York, was begun in April 1847, and completed only after a catastrophic collapse of the structure on 11 March 1848. This viaduct had four arches, and was 300 feet in length and 90 feet in height. At about noon, the entire viaduct, still encased with scaffolding, collapsed into the River Nidd. A deficient pier was held responsible, and the damage was estimated to be about £10,000.

Fortunately, the even bigger viaduct across the Crimple suffered no catastrophe similar to that which befell its sister over the Nidd. The great Crimple Viaduct is formed with 31 arches, each with a span of 50 feet, which uplift the track to a height of 110 feet.

It was built by the famous railway 'king', George Hudson, whose work was praised even at the time of construction. A contemporary lithograph in the Science Museum, South Kensington, dated August 1847, shows the viaduct, accompanied by the following description: 'This stupendous work is now erecting under the superintendence of J. C. Birkenshaw, Esq, C.E., It contains 31 arches of beautiful proportion and great height. The total length 1,873 feet; the main line from Leeds to Thirsk runs under the second arch, as shewn in the drawing, and thus is formed for future generations one of the most magnificent records of the skill and enterprise of the British nation in the 19th century.' The 20th century showed its understanding of this 'magnificent record' by closing the line from Pannal junction to Starbeck, as well as the whole of Bilton junction. Their re-opening, as part of a revived public transport system for the Harrogate District in the 21st century, is greatly to be desired.

The junction of Ripon Road and Parliament Street, *c.*1904, showing the Kursaal and Spa Rooms.

King Edward's Drive was still being developed when this view was taken *c.*1910.

High Harrogate's Mornington Crescent, once the site of the famous old Dragon Hotel.

Beulah Street, *c.*1913.

Samson Fox – genius inventor, captain of industry, patron of the arts, public benefactor, and Mayor of Harrogate

Samson Fox, as a subject for biography, is a gift to any writer, as his life was a rags to riches story which encompassed invention, industrial innovation, funding of the arts, friendship with the royal family, innumerable acts of public benefaction, a memorable law-suite with the celebrated author of Three Men in a Boat, and spectacular service as Mayor of Harrogate. On learning of his death in 1903, King Edward VII telegraphed his condolences to Harrogate, at the loss of their outstanding townsman. For even a brief account of Samson Fox, the writer's greatest problem is what to leave out, rather than what to include, so rich and fulfilled a life did he live.

Samson Fox was born on 11 July 1838, at Bowling, near Bradford. His father, Jonas Fox, was an 'overlooker' at a neighbouring textile mill, which Samson entered, on leaving school at the age of eight, and where he worked five half days a week. Later, in 1853, aged 15, Samson entered the Victoria Iron Foundry in Leeds, as an apprentice, an experience which confirmed his love affair with the two driving forces of 19th-century technology: iron and steam. This love affair had been obvious to his parents, who later recorded that when his father had wanted Samson to become a weaver, the lad had replied "I'll tramp till I find a job as a mechanic, and I'll have nowt else." On being told that as a budding weaver he was getting ten shillings a week, whereas he would only get five as a mechanic, he remained adamant, to his father's irritation, but his mother backed him, saying: "If he gets nowt, he's going to be a mechanic."

Throughout the late 1850s, Samson Fox obtained valuable experience in engineering and forging work, developing a reputation as a hard worker, although he still had time to meet and fall in love with a Knaresborough girl, Mary Ann Slinger, whom he married in May 1861. Stimulated by an 1862 visit to the great machinery exhibition in London, he promoted a company of his own, Fox Brothers & Reffitt, tool makers and hydraulic engineers, the success of which led to the launching of the Leeds Forge Company Ltd, with a nominal capital of £200,000, and whose first year's trading produced a loss of £538! But perhaps the single most important year in Fox's life was 1877, when he took out patents on his invention, the corrugated boiler flue. This was at a time when engineers were making ever greater demands on the energy producing power of the steam boiler, one result of which was to increase the number of boiler failures through the inability of the boiler flues to withstand the extra pressure. Fox found that by corrugating, or crinkling the flues, the same amount of metal became far stronger, thus reducing accidents and failures, and increasing efficiency.

Another patent provided for the manufacture of these corrugated boilers by means of rolling in a special mill. The first Fox patented boiler was sold in June 1877 to a Barrow shipyard, and from then onwards, there was no turning back. A period of frenzied work produced a breakdown, and March 1878 saw Fox convalescing in Harrogate, where he stayed at Beulah House in Chapel – today Oxford – Street. At this time Harrogate was being governed by men such as Richard Ellis and George Dawson, and was a hive of development, with an atmosphere of progress and growth which would not have been lost on the 40-year-old Fox. This was the beginning of a fruitful relationship between the exclusive little Yorkshire town and the brilliant business tycoon. With health restored by his Harrogate visit, Fox spent much of 1879 negotiating with Schultz Knaudt & Co of Essen whereby Fox's patents could be licensed in Germany, an agreement which was hugely successful for both parties. The outbreak of the Zulu War in

South Africa provided Fox with worldwide publicity when the steamer Pretoria, carrying the 91st Highlanders, reached South Africa from Great Britain after a record 24 days, six hours. The Pretoria was the first ocean-going steamship in the world to be fitted with the Fox corrugated boiler flue. Enriched by these successes, Fox decided to improve his social status and lifestyle, and removed from Leeds to Harrogate, where he purchased the World's End, a former inn, which was then named Grove House, beginning an ambitious programme of enlargement which eventually produced a residence fit for a king.

Grove House was turned into a residence of the greatest magnificence, which was subsequently described by the artist Bukovac:

"Never have I seen such riches. There was all the time a holiday feeling, and everything you could wish for was for you to take. Even a Prince would have been satisfied with my room. My bed was covered with silk, the blankets embroidered. Beside the bed was a bearskin with fine long hair, and all around, Persian carpets, also a wonderful silk table cover... In the fireplace huge logs burned and the big quiet flames were throwing a reddish light that merged with the gaslight white as sunshine. It was pleasant and warm, but outside the snowflakes fell slowly down. Some would stick to the glass, and then like molten jewels would slip down the pane. Reproductions of the greatest masters hung all round me... candlesticks from hand-beaten silver, ...a washbasin of crystal, with taps of hot and cold water.

"The bathroom adjoining was for myself alone and in it was only marble, silver and majolica. At 8 in the morning the manservant knocks; without a word (that is the English custom) he enters with a small tray on which is a silver plate with laced napkin and on it two thin slices of bread and butter, sugar and tea. All the vessels are from Royal Chinese porcelain. Having opened the window the manservant goes away to brush my suit and clean my clothes. After that, bowing, he announces

that breakfast is at 9.00 o'clock. From ten to noon I paint. At one o'clock is what we call main meal, that was lunch, and after it, a game of billiards or cards, and if the day was fine, tennis or golf. Automobiles were always ready to take us 50 or 60 miles, to another such town. There one drinks tea, 'five o'clock tea', a simple snack, then again into the automobile and by another route home.

"On return everyone goes into his room, takes a bath, changes into evening dress, as if for a ball. The meal that is 'dinner' is exactly at 7pm. One descends to the salon, where guests and family assemble. Gospodarica tells each gentleman which lady he should take into the dining room in line, pair by pair. Dvorana (a large hall) is decorated and brilliantly lighted, having in the middle a big table. In houses of richer Englishmen decoration of the table is an art – the gardener who grows all sorts of flowers, even orchids, is usually a clever artist himself.

"This Gospodska custom I liked very much. A man attired in dress coat and white tie feels much more noble at such a decorated, tasteful and rich table, where on each side tremble vessels of crystal and silver

and a cloth of pure lace reaches to the floor. In the midst of this is a great floral centrepiece, adorned with colourful ribbons. First, one drinks a glass of water, then immediately champagne, which is served to the end of the feast. When dinner is over, the ladies part from the gentlemen and retire to the salon, where conversation occurs while drinking black coffee, and when they get bored with that they move to the piano. But the gentlemen remain at table, where, together with coffee, old port or brandy is sipped. And so comes the time for anecdote and bigger jokes… Not ever did I expect the English to be so jolly… then to conversation, dancing and games. Later comes tea and snacks of all kinds. Some however hit whisky and soda, and so, up to bed…"

One aspect of Fox's cultural interest was his creation of the Leeds Forge Band, which informed opinion of the time judged to be the best brass band in the world. This was formed in 1882, and was often summoned to Harrogate to perform either at Grove House, or at more public locations. This same year also saw the issuing of patents for another brilliant Fox invention, the pressed steel railway bogie, which enabled freight wagons to be constructed from a single plate of pressed steel. The potential of this for the opening up of the US continental railroad systems, was not lost on Fox. He built a steelworks at Jolliet, Illinois, and employed his friend, Diamond Jim Brady to introduce the new wagon at the New York Trade Fair in 1888. A further fortune rolled in.

Fox developed his relationship with Harrogate through the 1880s. On 28 November 1885, he delivered a speech in the St James' Hall, Cambridge Street, on the causes of depression in trade, in which he came out as a keen advocate of protectionism. The same year saw him attending, with his son, Willie, the annual meeting of the Harrogate cricket club in Exchange Buildings, Parliament Street, at which Willie entertained the audience with a recital upon the violin. The *Advertiser* reported that the gentlemen of the club had received little Willie's recital with 'tears of rapture', although the rapture may in truth have been more the result of the father's offer to the club that they should 'consider his purse always open'. In 1886 Fox invited the great Croatian painter Bukovac to visit Grove House, which resulted in the acquisition by Fox of several masterpieces, one of which – Jesus and the children, later hung in St Robert's Church.

It was, however, the Ox roasting of 1887 which stamped itself indelibly on the public memory of Victorian Harrogate. This was to celebrate the Golden anniversary of Queen Victoria's reign. Fox invited the population of Harrogate to a party on High Harrogate Stray, at which an entire ox was roasted, and where free beer and buns were provided. The event was a brilliant success, and enjoyed unbroken sunshine. There were some 4,000 people present, and

Fox set up a dynamo on the Stray to illuminate the proceedings, which lasted well into the small hours. Fox repeated his generosity on two subsequent occasions: 1897, during Queen Victoria's Diamond Jubilee, and the end of the South African War, in 1902.

1887 also saw the great Wagnerian singer Nordica, about to perform Das Rheingold, seeking permission to visit the Leeds Forge, where no doubt the sight of tolling labourers would provide symbolic inspiration for the dwarfish Nibelungs working their ores within the depths of the Earth! This led to a meeting with Fox, and eventually to his undertaking to build the Royal College of Music, which now stands in Prince Consort Road, London, directly opposite the Royal Albert Hall. The project received powerful impetus when Sir George Grove, editor of Grove's Dictionary of Music, stayed at Grove House during Christmas 1887.

If one year could be taken as being typical of the life of Samson Fox, 1889 would be a good candidate. July saw the wedding at Bilton Church, of his daughter, Clara Louise, to Bernal Bagshaw, his chief engineer. The Leeds Forge Band played at Grove House, and the grounds were thrown open to a vast public celebration. The same month saw Queen Victoria's eldest grandson, Prince Albert Victor, visiting Harrogate to open the great national charitable institution of the Royal Bath Hospital, the rebuilding of which had been made possible largely through the generosity of Samson Fox.

To honour the Prince, Fox paid for the construction of two ornamental arches over the route the Prince would take from Grove House to the Royal Bath Hospital. The townspeople noted that although the arches were embellished with royal heraldic devices and patriotic flags, they were crowned by a replica of the device that had made all this possible – the Fox patented corrugated boiler flue! The visit of HRH Prince Albert Victor occurred two months after Samson Fox presented the Prince of Wales with a cheque for £45,000, during a dinner at Carlton House. This was the first of several payments which made possible the building of the Royal College of Music, one of the nation's great public institutions.

The year 1889 also saw the formation of Fox's 'Water Gas Syndicate' which promoted the use of the gas which is produced by blowing steam through beds of red-hot coke. To demonstrate the use of this gas, Samson Fox built Europe's first water gas street lighting plant, in Parliament Street, on the site later filled by the Royal Baths. The sensationally brilliant quality of the lighting caused the glass globes to be dubbed 'bottled suns'. Special trams from all over the north of England brought visitors into Harrogate to marvel at the wonder of the age. The water gas syndicate was not, however, a financial success, largely because water gas was more suited to use with welding, glass smelting, and metallurgical processes, than for public street lighting. Consequently, the syndicate failed, reducing many investors to ruin. When the author of *Three Men in a Boat*, Jerome K. Jerome, in an article published during 1897, accused Samson Fox of a deliberate scam, a law suite resulted.

Fox rounded off 1889 by winning an election as candidate for the council's East Ward. Finally, he was voted into the Mayoralty, a post he occupied until 1892. Throughout a phenomenally busy year, Fox added to the strength of his Leeds Forge Band, poaching six of the best players away from Black Dyke Mills Band. The following year, Fox expressed concern that Harrogate might not be keeping abreast of its rivals in the Spa business, and at his own expense, transported 13 members of the Council down to Bath, where he lodged them in the best hotel, before embarking on a thorough tour of the Bath Spa. Nor was this the only example of Fox's generosity.

On 17 July, Fox hired a special train, which was used to take Harrogate Corporation to London to witness the laying of the foundation stone of the Royal College of Music, by HRH The Prince of Wales. In the presence of a glittering assembly formed by the great and the good of the world's greatest city, Samson Fox, Mayor of Harrogate, handed the heir to the throne a special trowel, which – in a nice gesture – had been made from a corrugated boiler flue. One month later, almost as an afterthought, the Parliament Street water gas installation was switched on.

Samson Fox also interested himself in the preservation of old buildings, at a time when such interest was – to say the least – uncommon. When the beautiful building of the Old Victoria Baths, which once stood in Crescent Gardens, became redundant after the completion of the New Victoria Baths in 1871, the Council proposed its demolition.

Recognising its great architectural value, Samson Fox purchased it and removed the structure stone by stone, to his Grove House estate, where it was carefully re-erected, to form a laboratory and workshop. Here, Samson Fox installed his celebrated Holtzapfel lathe – on which he turned so many exquisite pieces – as well as an observatory for astronomical research. A further example of Fox's public spirit occurred when the old Dragon Hotel in High Harrogate was demolished. The entrance to the stables was a great stone arch, through which many a famous name had passed in the 18th and early 19th centuries, including Pagahini, when he played at the Dragon in 1833. Samson Fox saved the materials of the arch, and had them re-erected as part of his own new stables at Grove House, where they stand to this day.

So great was Samson Fox's contribution to Harrogate at this time, that when the fiftieth anniversary of the 1841 Harrogate Improvement Act came round in 1891, he staged a spectacular banquet in the grounds of Grove House. Three thousand Harrogate residents were invited, as well as the Lord Mayors of Leeds and Bradford, and after a splendid feast, the guests were entertained by the Leeds Forge Band, who played waltzes, gallops, quadrilles and Roger de Coverley's for the couples who danced through the night, a night made brilliant by a special water gas plant built in the grounds of Grove House. The great comedian, Dan Leno, was brought up from London, specially to entertain Mr Fox's guests, for which he was paid the then unheard of fee of one hundred pounds.

Another highlight came in 1894, when, on 2 May, the Prince of Wales opened the Royal College of Music, in the company of Princess Alexandra, 40 other members of the British and European Royal Families, members of the British Imperial Government, and many civic dignitaries. The climax of the celebrations occurred when Samson Fox, dressed in court costume with knee breeches, presented the Prince of Wales with a magnificent gold key, set with diamonds and emeralds, with which to open the new Royal College of Music building.

These years were, of course, the period of great debate in Harrogate about Richard Ellis's last great scheme, the building of the Royal Baths. After Ellis's death in 1895, his successor, Charles Fortune, became an energetic promoter of the Royal Baths project, but at the grand opening in 1897, Alderman Fortune told the visiting Duke of Cambridge, and the entire audience of assembled guests, that "it was entirely due to Mr Fox that the completion of the Royal Baths and Winter Gardens had been carried out in so magnificent a style."

No account of Samson Fox can be accurate without reference to his generosity to the poor and needy. Quite apart from his regular charitable funding, he also invited the poor of the neighbouring Smithy Hill into Grove House for food and entertainment. Secretly, he ordered his steward to provide deliveries of food and coal to the local poor, and his belief in sound affordable housing, led him to build cottages for workers in Starbeck, and also at Grove House.

A diabetic, Samson Fox's health became poor by about 1900, but his activities continued unabated. September 1903 saw him returning from the USA on the steamship Campania, his mind filled with thoughts a forthcoming Parliamentary election, but on 24 October, he died. On learning of his death, the Prince of Wales telegraphed Harrogate his deepest sympathy. Telegrams from Germany confirmed the high regard in which Samson Fox was held on the continent, especially at the firm of Schulz Knaudt, whose directors attended the funeral.

The service witnessed genuine expressions of

public grief, which was shared by the humblest of his employees, the same, perhaps, who had once met him at Harrogate station after his return from a successful business meeting in London, and had harnessed themselves to his carriage, dragging it home to Grove House, as a mark of affection. The *Harrogate Advertiser* published the revelation that Fox had, in great secret, distributed 'hundreds of tons of coal and beef to the Harrogate poor, and had even paid the rents and rates of the impoverished'. What John Motley wrote of the death of William of Orange, could well have been said on the death of Samson Fox: "As long as he lived, he was their guiding star, and when he died, the little children cried in the streets."

The truth about the water gas libel case only came out some 30 years after Fox's death. In the course of his memoirs, Alderman Frank Barber, who had been Fox's solicitor, admitted that as soon as Fox realised that the syndicate would fail, he spent much of his fortune in buying back shares from the smallest investors, in order to shield them from ruin.

The obituary of Samson Fox, published in the *Harrogate Advertiser*, contained an apt summary of his character:

His was a buoyant, hearty nature.

He was kind and generous of heart,

his will-power and indomitable energy were such as recognised no obstacle insurmountable.

Optimistic to a fault, his cheery influence and contagious

Hopefulness affected all with whom he came in contact.

If Samson Fox were alive at the time of writing, his affection for Harrogate would cause him to set up an investment trust to revive the Spa, and to further beautify and embellish what, in his own words, was "the bonny little town". Indeed, if Samson Fox had been born in any European country other than the United Kingdom, there would have been a statue erected long ago in honour of his memory. A statue to Samson Fox is long overdue, and Harrogate is the place for it. If Yorkshire business has any sense of pride in the achievements of past business pioneers, its leading names should foot the subscription list. Until that time, let us keep alive, and always honour, the memory of this great Englishman.

The story of the Harrogate Sun Pavilion

Origins of an amenity

The opening of the Sun Pavilion and its associated colonnade, on 17 June 1933, by Lord Horder, represented a stage in a process which had begun as early as 1778. In that year, the great 'Award' was made, which transferred from royal ownership to the people of Harrogate, the 'celebrated Mineral Wells' and the land on which they were situated. At the behest of the Duchy of Lancaster, the amount of land transferred to public use was far greater than the amount of land with identified mineral springs. There were two strong reasons for this generosity. First, it was believed that the known Mineral Wells represented only a portion of such phenomena in Harrogate, and that it was desirable to ensure that as many of the valuable medicinal wells as possible, passed into public control. Second, the medical profession had for centuries prescribed the use of Harrogate's Mineral Waters in conjunction with bodily exercise, either by means of walking, or riding, such exercise requiring open space in the vicinity of the Mineral Wells. However, the northerly situation of Harrogate meant that exercise had often to be undertaken under adverse weather conditions, which would either discourage the indolent, or prove harmful to the frail.

Improvements could only be introduced by the local doctors and innkeepers, or by the primitive authority maintained by the Township, and as the former spent their money by improving their own properties, and the latter was dominated by the doctors and innkeepers, it is not surprising that nothing was done on public land.

One part of the Stray – as the 200 acres came to be known – included Bogs Field, an oozing, bubbling marsh, covered by an ill-smelling miasma, and riddled with springs with various mineral properties. The establishment in 1824 of a great charitable hospital within yards of the Bogs Field, enabled the hospital to take advantage of the Mineral Wells, and led to investigations into their medical properties. At the same time, the public began to visit Bogs Field, walking along a footpath which ran from the Old Sulphur Well, where today stands the Royal Pump Room Museum.

This was the beginning of the Valley Gardens. The public in the early 19th century had rights of access to the Stray, which at Bogs Field was reached by Cornwall Road, and the Sulphur Well footpath. Throughout the 19th and 20th centuries, the town authority acquired more and more of the land between Bogs Field and the Old Sulphur Well, which began to take on the appearance of a pleasant garden. Trees, shrubs and flowers were planted, a pump room for the Magnesia Well was built in 1858, and more attention paid to the requirements of the visitors. The coming of the railway, in 1849, encouraged ever increasing numbers of visitors, a trend which grew dramatically, after the opening in 1862, of a new central railway station in Station Square.

In 1869, Richard Ellis, the greatest of mid-Victorian Harrogate's public servants, put forward a proposal to build a covered colonnade between the Royal Pump Room and the Royal Bath Hospital, for the purpose of providing a protective 'promenade' for

visitors wanting to exercise, as well as for people wanting to move between the two amenities. The Ellis proposal was given careful consideration by the Improvement Commissioners, being eventually deferred because of the more important proposal to build the New Victoria Baths, the foundation stone of which was laid by Ellis on 4 February 1871. The new baths – which were converted into the Council Offices in 1930 – included a covered walk along their frontage, which although far smaller than the Valley Gardens scheme, still acknowledged the need for a covered promenade. And there matters rested, at least from the point of the town's authorities.

Across Ripon Road, opposite the New Victoria Baths, the Spa Rooms, owned by a private business consortium, was undergoing a programme of improvement and enlargement. At its re-opening in 1871, the Spa Rooms provided its visitors with a splendid glazed promenade, or gallery, which ran along the entire north façade of the old 1835 building.

This glazed gallery was fronted on Ripon Road by a new Pump Room of iron and glass, the great dome of which soon became one of Victorian Harrogate's most photographed landmarks. Within, the waters of the world's strongest Chloride of Iron Well was dispensed, the fame of which was enhanced by the work of the internationally celebrated analytical chemist, Dr Sheridan Muspratt, whose Harrogate work on behalf of humanity, was praised by Charles Dickens.

The combination of medicinal mineral waters dispensed in an elegant pump room, connected to a great concert room and theatre, and a glazed walk for visitors to exercise and promenade their fashionable attire, proved hugely attractive, and the new amenities rapidly became Harrogate's leading attraction.

The later years of the 19th century saw many improvements in Harrogate, of which the most important, as well as spectacular, was the building of the Royal Baths. An especially admired feature of the 1897 structure was the Winter Garden, a glazed promenade with a height of 35 feet, a width of 42 feet and a length of 183 feet. The Winter Garden, the design of which must have been influenced by the successful additions to the Spa Rooms, soon became an important aspect of Spa life in Harrogate. Patients at the Baths could not only walk in it, but obtain amusement. Refreshments were provided, musical recitals programmed, and special events such as dances, 'fetes' and 'nocturnal illuminations', when the place was filled with potted palms and lit by thousands of tiny electric bulbs.

The Council did not neglect Valley Gardens, and in 1886 and 1902, the purchase of two parcels of privately-owned fields along Cornwall Road meant that the whole site of the modern Sun Pavilion and Colonnade was now in public ownership. 1895 saw the opening of a new pump room for the Magnesia Well – the present café – as well as a band stand and thatched tea house. It is hardly surprising to learn that the new amenities in Valley Gardens were also popular with patients and visitors to the neighbouring Royal Bath Hospital. The stage was set for the Valley Gardens as backdrop to the golden age of Edwardian Harrogate.

The battle to build

Up to the 1890s, visitors passing between the Royal Pump Room and the detached portion of Stray in Valley Gardens known as Bogs Field, were either visiting the Royal Bath Hospital or taking the air on Harlow Moor, the lower portion of which was purchased by the Corporation in 1898. Fewer of the visitors bothered to visit Bog's Field for the mineral waters, following the decision to pipe them down to the Victoria Baths, and then the Royal Baths, although the Magnesia Well Pump Room continued to be popular with visitors who had diuretic problems. All this changed, however, with the opening in 1895 of a new bandstand and tea house, both of which were located on virtually the same sites as their 1933 replacements. The Valley Gardens had been greatly improved in the years following Queen Victoria's Golden Jubilee of 1887, and by the time of the reign of Edward VII all facilities were in place that were necessary to ensure public popularity.

Reports in contemporary issues of the *Harrogate Advertiser* and *Harrogate Herald* show that the Elgar Walk became a very fashionable promenade in the years before World War One, with the cream of society displaying, with evident relish, their elaborate clothing; ladies with beautiful gowns and wide-brimmed hats – the so called Merry Widow Hats – long white gloves, and delicate veils, adding just the slightest hint of mystery. Gentlemen, with well-pressed morning coats and glossily burnished top hats, some carrying malacca canes, or perhaps pince-nez. Bath chairs were much in evidence, filled, invariably, with an old lady, usually large in stature and rich in circumstance, and pushed – also invariably – by a boy or old man, meagre in stature and poor in circumstance. The objective of these visitors was usually the band stand, where – throughout the season – music could be heard, accompanied on occasion by the minstrels, or Tom Coleman and his pierrots. The thatched tea house also provided refreshments, supplied under contract from local cafés and bakers.

During World War One, the tea house became a popular venue for officers recuperating in the Furness Home for Military Officers – as the Grand Hotel was for a time known. The Royal Bath Hospital, within 48 hours of the outbreak of war, placed itself at the disposal of the War Office, for the reception of convalescent and wounded soldiers and sailors, the first batch of which arrived in Harrogate on 4 December 1914. Indeed, a total of 692 men, including Canadians, Australians and Belgians, were received in the Royal Bath Hospital during the first year of conflict. The concentration of such a high number of Military personnel in both the Royal Bath Hospital and former Grand Hotel, turned the area between the two buildings – where the Sun Pavilion now stands – into a fascinatingly cosmopolitan scene, at least, during good weather. Later generations of Harrogate citizens have recalled the romantic attachments which developed between patients and local girls, and of the popularity of the thatched tea house as a meeting place.

After the ending of World War One, Harrogate believed it could simply pick up the pieces and return to the 'normal' conditions of 1914, but in reality it took the town some time to understand that the world had changed. No longer could the town rely on visits from a few very rich visitors to keep the Spa economy going, but instead, had to attract greater numbers of middle-income visitors.

A number of proposals for achieving this desirable goal were framed in the 1920s, of which the most comprehensive was the spectacular scheme of Alderman Barber. This called for the creation of a huge Roman forum in Crescent Gardens from which vehicular traffic would be excluded. The forum linked the Royal Baths, Royal Pump Room and New Victoria Baths with a new Spa Hall, by means of a covered colonnade through which visitors could exercise. The Barber scheme, costing an estimated million pounds, was too much for the Council to take on, but it succeeded in reviving the old idea of a covered walkway. As the 1920s progressed, British Spas experienced declining numbers of visitors, with Harrogate alone continuing to produce an annual profit.

Despite this, the Council decided to press on with schemes of improvement, both in order to keep their existing levels of business and also to be in a strong position to take advantage of the revival, when it came. A scheme was worked out by Alderman Sir Ernest Bain, with the help of Borough Engineer C. E. Rivers, Deputy Borough Engineer Leonard Clark – who was also a fine architect – and the General Manager of the Baths and Wells Department, Mr Broome. The scheme entailed the route of Cornwall Road being diverted, to go between the old Royal Pump Room and the back of the Crown Hotel, with the annex to the Royal Pump Room being demolished to make way for the road, which would have a gradient of 1 in 10.3, as against 1 in 8.2. The Valley Gardens would then be extended to take in the old Royal Pump Room, which in turn could be linked to a new development filling the site along Cornwall Road as far as the Royal Bath Hospital.

To be constructed in three stages, the new development consisted of (1) a new Pump Room, to be built on the Cornwall Road side of the land at the entrance to Valley Gardens; (2) a new Sun Pavilion, to replace the thatched tea house, which would be linked to the Royal Bath Hospital and the new Pump Room by a covered colonnade; and (3) a purpose built aviary, as a visitor attraction. This being Harrogate, it should be supererogatory to add that objections were not long in coming!

On Thursday 9 June 1932, in the Council offices, the Ministry of Health held an inquiry into Harrogate Council's Valley Gardens scheme, with many of the town's 39,785 residents being crammed into the public gallery as observers. Alderman Sir Ernest Bain outlined Harrogate's need to keep ahead of its Spa rivals, and the Borough Treasurer, James Stephenson, explained that the application was to borrow £22,500, the maximum term for repayment being estimated at 30 years. The annual loan charge would be £1,425, but with an estimated annual profit of £425 from the new Pavilion, the rate equivalent for the remaining £1,000 loan charge was only a halfpenny in the pound. Alderman Sir Ernest Bain added that the Council did not intend to build the whole scheme, estimated to cost £60,000, all in one go, but rather to proceed only with stage one, at an estimated £30,000.

Objectors fell into two categories; those who objected on grounds of expense, and those who objected to building along the south side of Cornwall Road. The former appeared to carry little, weight with the Inspector, Mr E. Butler, largely because Harrogate Council was virtually unanimous in its support for the scheme. The latter appeared a more formidable opposition, as it consisted of residents of Cornwall Road, whose properties were on long lease from the Duchy of Lancaster, with leases which included clauses regarding rights of southern light.

The opposition was represented by Mr E. A. Titley, a respected local solicitor, who appeared on behalf of David Simpson Estates, as well as individual residents. Mr Titley was, in the event, not helped by the habit of several of his clients, of shouting comments in the course of proceedings, to the evident annoyance of the Inspector. Mr Titley's principal case against the proposed development was that the building of the colonnade's rear wall along the south side of Cornwall Road, would affect adversely the view and light of the residents on the north side. Questioning the Borough Engineer, Mr Titley demanded to know how high the wall would be above the present hedge. Mr River's reply that because of the sloping nature of the site, and plans to lower the ground level on the Valley Gardens side, the wall would be, on average, one foot below the line of the hedge. This so nonplused the opposition, that it virtually collapsed. Adding a *coup de grace*, Mr Rivers pointed out that the only substantial height occurred with the proposed Sun Pavilion, which was to be sited opposite the homes of no residents, but rather the enormous Grand Hotel!

Support for the proposed scheme came from the Chamber of Trade, and from the powerful Medical Society, whose representative, Dr W. Edgecombe, described the plans as 'one of the best-proposed improvements for the last 35 years" – i.e. since the opening of the Royal Baths. One point to be made again and again, was that improvements were needed for the provision of band recitals. The old, circular, open bandstand was fine when the sun shone, but wind or rain made it unusable, and the gardens emptied of visitors when the weather broke. The new bandstand, placed opposite a large tea room and lounge – the proposed Sun Pavilion – would guarantee regular programming. Eventually the Inspector found in the Council's favour, but pointed out that his ruling applied only to the first stage of the proposals – which were the building of the Sun Pavilion and Colonnade – and not to the other stages, which should be subjected to separate inquiries.

Work on the Valley Gardens improvements began immediately the inquiry was over, and such good progress was made that the new Sun Pavilion and Colonnade were ready for public use by Whitsuntide 1933.

The Opening of the Sun Pavilion

The completion of the Sun Pavilion and Colonnade in the spring of 1933 was regarded with some pride, especially as it had been built in the face of the worst depression in living memory, and a deteriorating situation in Europe. To mark the occasion, Harrogate Council invited Lord Horder of Ashford, KCVO, and physician to the Prince of Wales, to perform the ceremonial opening. Civic guests of the Mayor & Mayoress of Harrogate, Alderman and Mrs Whiteoak, included the Lord Mayors of Hull, and York, and the Sheriff of York, the Mayors of Morley, Todmorden, Batley, Brighouse, Richmond, Ripon, Scarborough, Doncaster, Halifax, Huddersfield, Bridlington, the Chief Constable of the West Riding of Yorkshire, the

Chairman of the County Council, the president of the Harrogate Medical Society, Dr Laura Veale, Major. The Rt Hon J. W. Wills, MP, and Freemen J. R. Ogden and Alderman Shepherd. Other guests included all the Harrogate Town Council, the chief officers, the contractors and leading members of the British Medical Profession.

The official programme began with the meeting of the London Medical party at a specially decorated Harrogate Railway Station, by Dr Veale, followed by luncheon at the Grand Hotel. The Mayoral party, with Lord Horder, and followed by the representatives from the Magistrates Bench, marched from the Council Offices, through Valley Gardens, escorted by the Claro Division Police and the band of the Seaforth Highlanders. On arriving at the Sun Pavilion, the Mayoral party took up its position with the Medical party, and the Mayor of Harrogate welcomed the guests to the town's magnificent new Sun Pavilion. Lord Horder began his speech with the observation that he was "glad to see that the premier Spa of Great Britain is determined to maintain the prestige which it has so worthily held in the past", and continued "nature has been lavish in her endowments to your town and to your county. You, on your part, have not failed in your duty by adding to them the benefits of science and the embellishments of art. All of these things are necessary if you aim at making Harrogate an asylum for men and women who are tired and jaded by modern city life, and a place where the sick and disabled may find healing and restoration". In his response the Mayor reminded his guests that Lord Horder had won distinction in his profession, winning in one year, gold medals for work in medicine, surgery and midwifery – a rare honour – and that he has treated three Prime Ministers in turn, Bonar Law, Lloyd George and Ramsay MacDonald.

The day ended with a banquet given by Harrogate Corporation and the Harrogate Medical Society, in the Winter Garden of the Hotel Majestic, where guests in full evening dress were serenaded with a recital of English music, played by the Royal Baths Quartet under the direction of Mr Cecil Moon. After the banquet, the toasts were given, including one from the Mayor, who – with perhaps more enthusiasm than wisdom – told the Mayor of Scarborough that if Harrogate had the sea, Scarborough could "shut up shop!" Lord Horder's speech contained some interesting suggestions about the introduction of 'Kur, or cure, Taxes', to be levied on all visitors for the use of the town's Spa amenities. This was also one of Alderman Barber's pet subjects. It was when he came to the matter of road traffic, that Lord Horder became quite warm. He advised the assembled dignitaries that Harrogate, in attempting to please both the invalids and the hooligans – i.e. motorists – was doomed to failure. To laughter and applause, Lord Horder

remarked "It is obvious you have power to shut down traffic along certain thoroughfares at certain hours of the day. I would go the whole hog, and restrict traffic to 6 or 8 miles per hour in the town centre. Send all of them round the town and be dammed to them. Motor traffic and invalids should not be mixed."

Along with Civic dignitaries, the guests included many eminent names from the world of business and medicine, including Sir Montague Burton, Sir A. W. MacIntosh, Sir Henry J. Buckland – former manager of Harrogate's Wells and Baths, and now General Manager of the Crystal Palace – and Sir H. F. Bruce Bruce-Porter. A series of magnificent bouquets were presented to female guests, but in the process an error occurred, which resulted in the Superintendent of Police presenting the burly figure of the Town Clerk, Mr J. Turner Taylor, with an immense bunch of pink carnations!

The publicity given to the new Sun Pavilion and Colonnade made much of the special glass with which the walk-ways were roofed, reminding readers that it admitted only those rays of the sun which were healthful, excluding anything of a harmful nature. One early visitor was reported as being most favourably impressed by Harrogate's latest improvement – the Queen. Queen Mary visited Harrogate with her daughter, the Princess Royal and Countess of Harewood, on 25 August 1933. The two Sun Parlours became popular with elderly visitors, on account of their being heated for the elaborate potted plants which were grown there. But it was the main Sun Pavilion which enjoyed the greatest success with the public, due in no small part to the regular provision of music and other entertainments, and the provision of a high class café. In view of this success, the abandonment by the Council of the next two stages of the development – the new Pump Room, and the aviary with connecting link to the Royal Bath Hospital – may seem surprising. However, there was a very good explanation for this.

In December 1932, the Director of Parks had – with the approval of his Chairman – cut into the Stray at West Park, in order to construct a flower bed. The public uproar produced by this action, instead of discouraging the Council from meddling with the Stray, seemed to encourage them to affirm and extend it. The public, incensed by the Council's wilful refusal to come to terms with the widespread hostility to the Stray scheme, eventually lost patience, and a Stray Defence Association sprang into being, which stood for election against the established candidates, and swept the board. The new Councillors, in 1934, scraped the hated and undoubtedly illegal flower beds, restored the Stray, and then set about the less controversial matter of running Harrogate. At least where financial investment was concerned, the new Council had weaker nerves than its predecessor, and in consequence, decided to abandon the next two stages of the Valley Gardens development. The moral for the Council is clear in this story: you can do nearly anything you want in Harrogate, so long as you leave the Stray alone!

It was the fashion in the 1930s for resorts to emphasise their amenities for health, sport and fresh air, and Harrogate was no exception to this practice. The new Sun Pavilion fitted into this lifestyle beautifully, and was incorporated with many posters and booklets, thus becoming a familiar aspect of the public image of Harrogate. To sit within the glazed colonnade, overlooking the immaculately maintained Valley Gardens, while listening to the playing of Roland Powell and his fellow musicians, was an agreeable pastime which proved irresistible to visitors. The café service was faultless, with tables being dressed with fine linen, and good quality china and cutlery. And people expected no less. This, after all, was Harrogate. Indeed, when the 1930s came to their abrupt end in August 1939, with the outbreak of World War Two, the Council kept the place open, and the *Harrogate Advertiser* published a special weekly column of events at the Sun Pavilion.

Throughout World War Two, the Sun Pavilion formed a little beacon of relaxation in a Harrogate darkened by the cares of the times. On 14 February 1940 the *Herald* reported that the Council had agreed that the Sun Pavilion would not be blacked out, and the edition for 3 July 1940 referred to it as 'a miniature oasis of gaiety and pleasure in a war-ridden world'. If the Sun Pavilion belonged in the 1930s to the visitors, the 1940s saw its adoption by the residents. In one extraordinary period in 1941, morning coffee was provided for the combined talents of the Royal Opera House Covent Garden, the Old Vic Company, and the Sadlers' Wells Opera Company, in Harrogate from 4 August until early September. Sybil Thorndike exchanged pleasantries with Walter Widdop, Joan Cross exchanged opinions with Lawrence Collingwood. Talk was of King John, Euripides 'Medea', and of operas such as Hansel and Gretel, Traviata, and Figaro. Days later, Margot Fonteyn and Frederick Ashton were in the Pavilion, probably discussing conductor Constant Lambert's handling of Giselle, Les Sylphide, and Swan Lake – all being staged in the Kursaal for the delight of Harrogate's wartime audiences. Unbelievable – yes, but it happened, nevertheless.

The post-war world brought many changes to Harrogate, with the decline of the Spa, the rise of the exhibition and conference business, but the Sun Pavilion survived throughout the 1940s, 1950s and 1960s as a delightful venue in which to meet family and friends, to relax with light refreshment and listen to the band, or just watch the birds, as they flew through the open windows, attracted by the cake crumbs from the tables. Special events were mounted in the main Pavilion. Dances, band recitals, charity shows, exhibitions, displays – all were accommodated, and all continued to attract the public. Many Harrogate people still recall, with pleasure and gratitude, the performances of Doris Nixon on the organ, at 3pm every afternoon, save Sundays and Mondays; Stanley Greaves and Julie (Thursday Night is family night); Barbara Simpson and Ernest Clough and their *Wednesday Rendezvous*, or 'Friday Night is Music Night', 'with a galaxy of Stars', and, to close the week, Tom Harrison and his 'Olde Tyme Music Hall', complete with old time dancing. In 1974, ticket prices ranged from 11p to 35p – value indeed. Remember, too, the Sunday afternoon Brass Band concerts, and, in the summer months, Clary Wilson's 'Serenade on a summer's evening', with the Sun Pavilion Orchestra.

The 1970s witnessed a gradual change in council attitudes towards maintaining the town's historic buildings. The Tewit Well, England's oldest Spa, in continual use since 1571, fell into decay in 1971, being very nearly demolished. The Royal Hall, Royal Pump Room and Royal Baths were neglected, and took on a shabby and forlorn, appearance. The market began to show its age, and the Western Wing of the Royal Baths began to deteriorate seriously. Both of these two last buildings had been designed by the same architect, Leonard Clark, who had also designed the Sun Pavilion, and indeed the Sun Pavilion used similar methods of construction, with artificial stone, brick, and a steel frame. Consequently, council neglect of the Sun Pavilion produced problems similar to the neglected market and Royal Baths Western Wing. Water penetration damaged the frame, which rusted and harmed the surrounding artificial stone. A foolish cost cutting regime lowered standards at the Sun Pavilion. First, the table cloths went, being replaced with horrid little plastic topped tables. Then waitress service was abolished, with plastic roll-topped counters taking their place, with all the glamour of a seedy transport cafe. Then, selective opening hours were introduced, which meant that the Pavilion only opened when the management believed there would be custom. So on a fine day, the public would turn up in droves, to find the Sun Pavilion closed. Needless to say, the public turned elsewhere, and – with declining income – further cuts were made. Staff were reduced, painting and repairs postponed, cleaning done less frequently. It was all very sad, and gave strength to the prevailing belief that late twentieth century councils were simply incapable of running a business.

A year after the prestigious new Conference Centre opened in 1981, the Sun Pavilion closed. The announcement was made by the Director of Resort Services, Tony Miles, being published in the *Advertiser* for 4 June 1982. It was followed by a flood of letters, many of them angry, in which residents and visitors alike took the council to task for permitting the Sun Pavilion to close. And then the really dangerous suggestion was made, which is always made whenever a council finds itself with a nearly derelict building on its hands – turn it into an art gallery or museum. The *Advertiser* for 4 November 1983 carried the official suggestion! together with news that a working party had been set up.

On 24 June 1985 the committee reported to the Conference & Leisure Services Group, mentioning sums of between £85,000 and £805,925, required to implement the various options. A row broke out in Council about the handling of the matter, which was reported in the *Advertiser* for 28 June 1985, alongside letters from visitors from Sheffield and Blackpool urging Harrogate to put its house in order.

Public interest in the Sun Pavilion and Colonnades became focused in 1986 with the setting up of the Friends of the Valley Gardens, thanks to the determination of resident Mrs Anne Smith, a member of the Harrogate Society, which also backed the new group. A 12- strong committee included Les Olend, the recently retired head of Leeds Parks Department, and Geoffrey Smith, the famous TV gardener. James Wight, better known as James Herriott, also joined the Friends, and added his own influential voice to those clamouring for the restoration of the Sun Pavilion, as did his co-patron, Professor David Bellamy.

During the next ten years, the Sun Pavilion was seldom out of the newspapers, with a huge amount being written and published on the subject. 1987 was an especially busy year, which saw publication of the interesting proposal to convert the Sun Pavilion into a nightclub – a suggestion which produced a stormy reaction.

Faced with such a high level of vocal public concern over the fate of the Sun Pavilion, the Council attempted to find a solution which would allow the building to be restored without placing an impossible, half-million pound, burden on local rate payers. On 3 October 1986, the *Advertiser* published details of the Council's brief for developers, which included allowance for converting part of the Cornwall Road section of Valley Gardens into a car park. This unleashed a storm of protest, which proved a godsend to the Council's political opponents A ten-year-old schoolboy, Julian Hall, began a petition against the scheme, which raised 1,000 signatures within a week. The Harrogate Society opposed the scheme. On 5 December, 1986, the *Advertiser* announced that they had received a letter from James Herriot, the famous Yorkshire vet and writer, which roundly condemned the car parking scheme. However, the scheme was not opposed unanimously. Councillor Rodney Kent described it as being 'pragmatic', and – incredibly – the town's member of Parliament, Robert Banks, in referring to the proposed Valley Gardens car park, said "It might turn out to be a bonus".

The Friends of Valley Gardens, under the energetic leadership of Mrs Ann Smith, presented the public with a number of interesting options for the future of the Sun Pavilion, including its conversion into an indoor tropical garden, similar to the famous Canal Gardens at Leeds.

Meanwhile, the North of England Horticultural Society, who had used Valley Gardens as the venue for their Spring Flower Show since 1934, had been feeling the constraints of the Gardens, owing to the success and expansion of their annual exhibitions. Accordingly, they drew up plans to work in conjunction with the Borough Council, and to refurbish the Sun Pavilion and colonnades, to create a permanent base for the Flower Shows, and to provide further amenities within Valley Gardens, such as Conservatories. In all, the Society looked to spending some £1,350,000 over a four-year period. Almost from the first publication of the North of England Horticultural Society's proposals, disquiet was expressed by those members of the public who believed that the plans were too intensive, that they would split the gardens, and create insuperable problems with coach and car parking at peak periods. The NEHS put forward a series of proposals, which ranged from minimum alteration to the Valley Gardens, to a quite extensive programme of construction and remodelling, and although their proposals were obviously geared to meeting the interests of the Society, they were well thought-out, carefully presented, and backed by sound financial resources.

Other schemes were also in the offing. Dr Joe Friend published proposals in 1987 to convert the Sun Pavilion into a sauna, and Leeds businessman Sydney Marsh proposed a quality coffee lounge and restaurant, with staff wearing '18th-century Regency costume (!!), as well as a tropical butterfly house. More ominously, in November 1987, the Council removed the glazed roof from the neglected Sun Colonnades, thus guaranteeing the maximum penetration of the structure by rain. At the same time, the NEHS proposals, designed by the Glen Kemp Hankinson partnership, Landscape Architects & Planning Consultants, were published. They were treated to extensive public comment, in the pages of the *Advertiser*, as were the alternative proposals of the Friends of Valley Gardens. The talking continued throughout 1988 and 1989, and by September 1989, the *Advertiser* carried news that the Sun Pavilion had deteriorated to the point that is was now too dangerous to be used for the 1990 Spring Flower Show, and would have to be boarded up. After a number of false starts, several more counter-proposals (including an aquarium and plant centre) and innumerable letters from the public complaining of inertia, the crunch had arrived.

It was now or never. In March 1990, the Council took the decision to spend £145,000 on repairing the Sun Colonnade and two Sun Parlors, by means of removing the remaining glazing, and repairing the brick and artificial stone structure. Although nothing was to be done with the decaying Sun Pavilion, this was a move in the right direction. And it was a move which had been made possible by the overwhelming public opinion in favour of restoration.

As work progressed on the Sun Colonnades, discussions continued on the vexed question of how to rescue the Sun Pavilion. On 24 January 1992, the *Advertiser* carried details of the handing back to the Council of the Sun Colonnades, by contractor Arthur Stephenson, an event which stimulated further letters from the public demanding action over the Pavilion, which since its boarding up, had become increasingly derelict and vandalised. The extent of this dilapidation was evident when, after precautions for public safety had been taken, the building was opened temporarily in August 1994, to exhibit a gigantic statue by David Mach, assembled from piles of newspapers. Meanwhile, the Council was preparing a submission for restoration funds from the new National Lottery, and on 24 November 1995, the *Advertiser* announced that a £403,000 grant had been made by the lottery, for the purpose of restoring the Sun Pavilion.

Commenting on the award, Council Leader Phil Willis said: "I get more letters about this building than anything else," and that the building was "a symbol of all that was good about the 1930s 1940s and 1950s". A set-back to these proposals occurred in August 1996 when an arson attack caused extensive damage to the dome, requiring the presence of fire fighters from as far away as Acomb and Ripon. Then, at long last, on 24 April 1997 work began on the restoration of the Sun Pavilion, funded by two National Lottery grants, totalling £440,000, plus a £20,000 grant matched by Harrogate Council, plus a £97,000 insurance payout, following the 1996 fire. The start of the work of restoration was attended by Adrian Jackson Associates, who had won the tender for the refurbishment of the building, and Mr Pat Fitzgerald, Director of Technical Services. In a nice touch, Barbara Simpson, the renowned local entertainer who had begun her career at the Sun Pavilion, with the Walter Garrard Orchestra, was also present.

The provision of Lottery funding was dependent on the restored building being available for a high degree of community use, and in March 1998, the Council considered the following usage: Community events & activities = 40%; School & Educational use = 5 per cent; Arts related events = 20 per cent; Commercial activities = 35 per cent.

Following the splendid restoration of the building, which included a much admired new entrance from Cornwall Road, there arrived the crowning moment for its formal re-opening. This occurred on 10th December 1998, when Queen Elizabeth declared the Sun Pavilion open, unveiling a commemorative plaque to mark the occasion. In company with the Mayor of Harrogate, Councillor Ruth Timmis, and guests, the Queen attended a reception which included a dance demonstration, all of which took place beneath the pavilion's glowing stained glass dome. Once again, the Sun Pavilion took its place as one of the sights of Harrogate.

The Yorkshire Princess and Harrogate

'The Yorkshire Princess, 1897-1965' was the title of the 1997 exhibition shown at Harewood House, which commemorated the life of Princess Mary, the Princess Royal, who lived at Harewood for 35 years. Princess Mary was born in 1897 as the third child and only daughter of the Duke and Duchess of York (later, King George V and Queen Mary); her brothers were David (later King Edward VIII) and Bertie (later King George VI). On 28 February 1922, Princess Mary married Lord Lascelles, son of the 5th Earl of Harewood, the couple moving Goldsborough Hall, a few miles from Harrogate, thus opening a long and fruitful association between the Princess and the town.

The *Harrogate Advertiser* announced that Princess Mary had visited Harrogate on 21 August 1922. The Princess must have enjoyed her visit, as she returned the following year on 16 August in the company of her formidable mother, Queen Mary. The two must have been especially interested in the progress on the new War Memorial rising up in Prospect Square, especially as it was due to be unveiled by the Princess's husband, Lord Lascelles, in 15 days time. All Harrogate was present at this most solemn and memorable occasion, and the accompanying photograph shows Princess Mary on Pier Head, next to Lord Lascelles, the Mayor and Mayoress, Mr & Mrs David Simpson, and the Town Clerk, John Turner Taylor – in the background, the Café Imperial, today, Betty's.

1924 saw Princess Mary becoming a member of the Harrogate Lodge of the order of Foresters, and her reception of Queen Mary at Goldsborough Hall, reached via Harrogate. The following February, the Princess welcomed her brother, the Prince of Wales, to Goldsborough, and on 10 August 1924, she performed her first official duty in Harrogate by opening the laboratory of the Royal Bath Hospital in Cornwall Road, the last remnants of which are being erased as these words are set down. Nine days later, the Princess once again escorted Queen Mary round Harrogate. At this time the Princess began her long patronage of the Harrogate shops, one of which included Woods Linens.

During the terrible years of World War One, Princess Mary had trained as a nurse for sick children at the Great Ormond Street Hospital, and throughout her life, she took special interest in the welfare of the sick. It was therefore appropriate that when Harrogate planned to replace its old Cottage Hospital in Avenue Road, Princess Mary was involved; she laid the foundation stone of the new Knaresborough Road General Infirmary on 3 September 1926, and opened the re-named General District Hospital on 17 September 1932, eight months after King George V had conferred on her the title of Princess Royal.

Following the death of the 5th Earl on 6 October 1929, Lord Lascelles became 6th Earl, his wife becoming Countess of Harewood. The family moved from Goldsborough Hall into Harewood House, shortly after the new Earl had opened the Harrogate Art Gallery on 9 January 1930. In August 1933, King George and Queen Mary were in Harrogate, and on 25 August, the Princess Royal showed her mother, Queen Mary, the splendid new Sun Pavilion in Valley Gardens.

During World War Two the Princess Royal had to endure the knowledge that her son George, a Grenadier Guardsman, having been wounded, was a prisoner in Colditz Castle. Shortly after the end of the war, the Princess Royal lost her husband; the 6th Earl died in 1947, on 23 May, the same year as the couple's silver wedding anniversary. The Princess Royal lived on at Harewood until her death in 1965. In her speech on being made a Freeman of the Borough of Harrogate on 10 April 1951, the Princess Royal recorded her feelings for the place: "If I could choose anywhere in the world to live it would be here, the best place. My love for this part of Yorkshire has become such an integral part of my life that it would be a great sorrow for me to contemplate making my home elsewhere."

Gas showrooms

In the early years of the present century, the showrooms of the Harrogate Gas Company were located in Cambridge Road, but in 1918 they moved into larger premises in James Street, the site of which they continued to occupy until 1998. The annual reports of both the Harrogate Electricity and Gas companies show that unlike many other Yorkshire communities, that of Harrogate needed little persuading to adopt new forms of energy, although certain appliances – such as gas refrigerators – never became as popular as their electrical counterparts.

The James Street building into which the Gas Company had moved in 1918, was rebuilt in the later years of the 1920s in the classical revival style of the period, being an exact contemporary of the handsome Boot's building in Cambridge Street, to which it was connected at first-floor level by means of a bridge across back James Street. It was typical of the imaginative marketing adopted by the Gas Company that the top floor of their new James Street premises included a demonstration area where audiences of more than one hundred people could see girls of the newly introduced 'Home Economist' staff, cook with gas appliances. These demonstrations were very popular, and it may be that there are some readers who can remember being present at one of them.

During World War Two, the basement of the James Street building was converted into a NAAFI for visiting servicemen, was run by volunteers and provided – naturally – with a good gas fire. The accompanying photograph shows a gas cookery demonstration taking place in the window of the James Street building, c.1935. A group of passing ladies watch through the window, behind whom may be seen the premises of Baine's, precursor to Preston's. [Supplied by Management of British Gas Energy Centre]

The Avenue Hotel, at the corner of Victoria Avenue & Station Parade, *c.1935*.

A float of Britannia and attendants, when the English were not reticent in expressing pride in their nation and its achievements.

East Parade houses overlooked Sheepshanks' Field when this view was taken *c.*1910

Charles Dickens stayed at Binns' Hotel, Cold Bath Road, before it was renamed Lancaster.

Off for a spin – from Clifton College

Nineteenth-century guide books to Harrogate contain fulsome references to the town's excellent private schools, some of which appear to have been established. in the 18th century as a convenience for wealthy families visiting the Spa. One such was established at Grove House on World's End – today Skipton – Road, where Barbara Hofland, author of the fascinating *Season at Harrogate*, took up the headship in May 1809.

By the time of the 1833 *Harrogate Guide Book*, there were four such private schools listed; two for boys and two for girls. The proliferation of such establishments did not occur until the expansion of the 1860s, when, according to the historian William Grainge, 'few places of the same size are so well supplied with schools as Harrogate. Private boarding and day schools, for youth of both sexes, are numerous.' This postcard view shows one of Clifton College's buildings in Tewit Well Road, just round the corner from the main premises on Stray Road, opposite the Tewit Well.

Clifton College seems to have first opened in Queen Parade, and an advertisement of 1900 states that it was a boys' school which included 'Indian and Colonial' boys. In other words, boys of families in Indian and Colonial service. In 1906 the college removed to one of the new mansions erected in the early 1900s by Isaac Pickard, on Stray Road. The card dates from about 1910, and shows pupils setting out for a bicycle ride. Clifton closed in July 1968, the main building being subsequently demolished and replaced with the present block of flats. The building in this photograph still survives. [Supplied by Mr D. Lewis]

Harrogate's newest oldest hotel

After its opening in April 1999, a constant stream of visitors called at the Cedar Court Hotel on Park Parade, not for the purpose of booking accommodation, nor indeed for dinner in the elegant restaurant, but rather for the simple purpose of satisfying curiosity. These visitors had one thing in common, despite their differences of age. The younger ones knew the building from the time between 1951 and 1996, when it served as headquarters for the Regional Health Authority. Older visitors had memories of the building during World War Two, when it served as a personnel reception for the RAF, and some even remembered it in its original state as one of Harrogate's great hotels. According to which historian is consulted, the former Queen Hotel was erected as Harrogate's first custom built inn, either in 1671 or 1687. Before this time, visitors to Harrogate's famous Spa were accommodated at local farm or lodging houses, or – during the height of the 'season' when Harrogate was full – they stayed in other localities such as Beckwithshaw, Knaresborough, Otley or Wetherby. Certainly by the end of the 17th century, there were four large inns in High Harrogate – the Queen, the Granby, the Dragon and the Salutation. This last establishment survives today as the County Inn, but

the Dragon had closed by about 1890, being subsequently demolished to make way for Mornington Crescent, and the Granby is today a beautifully maintained residential home.

It is all the more satisfying, therefore, to report that High Harrogate once again has a great hotel, and that the new Cedar Court, established in the shell of the old Queen Hotel, is continuing the tradition of the famous 17th-century establishment. Here, Blind Jack, the Yorkshire road maker, entertained guests in the ballroom with his fiddle playing; here, the poet Thomas Gray, took shelter in 1762 as he 'passed over the ugly moor of Harrogate'; here, Lord Roberts, victor of the South African Wars, paraded through the front grounds, cigar in hand, to the plaudits of the assembled Harrogate crowds; here, the Duke and Duchess of Westminster stayed regularly, spending part of their vast fortune in the process; here, members of the Imperial Russian family stayed, during the golden years of Edwardian Harrogate. Many of the public spaces through which these notables once moved, may still be seen, for the great ballroom, the multi-columned dining room and the former reading room, all survived the major rebuilding of 1988. The illustration shows the Queen's Head in c.1790.

Harrogate's Floral Queen

Years of drab war and post-war austerity were banished from Harrogate on 2 September 1950 when a special gala day was held as part of the town's 'Fete and Gala Carnival'. The whole event had been organised by the Corporation's entertainments manager, W. W. Baxter. The gala programme began at 1.30pm, with a carnival procession through the town, attended by a large number of children. Other activities included 'keep fit' displays, a 'sensational high diving and comedy trampolinists aqua show of great perfection' by the Safto brothers, a 'Toy Town Tattoo' by staff and students of the Army Apprentices School, a motor-cycle gymkhanaa, and a recital by the Band of the Royal Artillery. A grand boxing tournament was presented by Harold Styan, and the children had a fun fair on West Park Stray. The celebrations concluded with a magnificent firework display provided by Standard Fireworks Ltd.

The highlight of the day, however, was undoubtedly the crowning of the town's 'Floral Queen'. The search for the ideal candidate for Harrogate's 'Floral Queen' appears to have been a thorough one, with several rounds of contest and elimination. At the finals, held in the Sun Pavilion on 7 August, the town's ten prettiest schoolgirls were interviewed by a panel of five, chaired by BBC producer Barney Colehan. The award of Floral Queen was given to the prettiest girl with the most engaging personality, the winner being the14-year-old Audrey Nathan, whose maids of honour were Sylvia Maltby (14), and Eileen Lunn (13), with Sandra Hardy, Margaret Righton, Pauline Pitt, Gillian Amy, Barbara Wright, Judith Ruddy, Eileen Johnson and Denise Stevenson as attendants.

At 2.15pm, the Floral Queen's procession left the Royal Baths, and entered Crescent Gardens, where, at 2.20pm, Audrey Nathan was crowned Floral Queen by the Mayoress of Harrogate, Mrs C. E. Whiteley. The procession then continued through the town, via King's Road, Cheltenham Mount, Commercial Street, Oxford Street, Cambridge Road, Prospect Square, West Park, and on to the Yorkshire Show Ground, where the Fete and Gala was opened by the Mayor, Alderman C. E. Whiteley. The accompanying photograph, kindly supplied by the former Miss Nathan's son, Russell Davidson, shows the Floral Queen at the Cenotaph, with her two pages, Martin Fenwick and Clive Kent, surrounded by a large and goodnatured crowd, the vast majority of which – let it be remembered – had just experienced the horrors of World War Two.

The Children's Library

Harrogate's public library services began well after what today is called 'the private sector', first began such facilities for subscribers. Back in the later 18th century, Eli Hargrove had offered a subscription service for visitors to his 'toy shop' in Church Square, and this was followed by Blackburn's Library, which operated from Library House on Regent Parade. The first 'free', or public library service, did not arrive in Harrogate until some time after the passing of the 1850 Public Libraries Act. Largely at the urgings of Charles Fortune throughout the 1870s, Harrogate Council finally agreed to adopt the Public Libraries Acts in 1886, opening a public reading room in Fern Villa, Princes Street.

From that time, Harrogate's public library movement never looked back, and in 1906, it moved into its present Victoria Avenue premises in the newly completed section of Alderman Fortune's planned 'gigantic Municipal Palace'. In those days, special library services for children were the exception, rather than the rule, largely because of the financial limitations of the permitted penny rate, not abolished until 1919. However, by the time of Harrogate Library's diamond jubilee in 1947, the necessity was recognised of providing an adequate facility for children. At this time, Harrogate Corporation had the great good fortune to employ the services of a remarkable man, John Stuffins, who was not only responsible for the town's library, but also its art and museum collections.

Despite the very difficult conditions of those immediate post-war years, Mr Stuffins managed to provide a children's library in the basement of the Victoria Avenue building, adapting a former storage area for the purpose. The photograph shows the opening, on April 8 1949, of the new Children's Library, by the Mayoress Mrs C. J. Simpson, flanked at left by Mrs A. Turner, and at right by Borough Librarian John Stuffins. The seated lady may be Mrs R. G. Paver-Crow. As for the three boys, two of them, David Lawrence and Colin Gibson, attended the 50th anniversary party held on Saturday 10 April 1999, when a party for today's younger generation was provided, with games, food and stories. It is good to report that the Children's Library services go on from strength to strength, having a large and appreciative membership.

The Old Bell Tavern

The name of the Old Bell Tavern may at first appear to be a fanciful piece of marketing hype, but in fact, the sign of the Bell in 1999, returned to its original site after a gap of 184 years. The Bell seems to have its origin in an early 17th-century ale house which served visitors resorting to Harrogate's famous Old Sulphur Well, which today lies directly opposite, beneath the dome of the Royal Pump Room.

According to the *York Courant* of 1768, Joseph Hogg, landlord of the Bell Tavern, had been accused of murdering one of his customers, but the edition for 21 June reported, in the direct language of the day: 'There does not appear to have been the least foundation for such a rumour, and the report has been solely owing to the distempered brain of a woman, who many years ago when big with bastard child, imposed greatly upon the public under the pretext of sympathy.'

Sometimes known as the Blue Bell, on account of its blue coloured sign, the Bell was a stage on the York to Harrogate coaching inn, the *York Courant's* advertisement of 27 May 1777 announcing: 'The York and Harrogate machine will begin from Mr Featherstone's, the White Swan, York, and go to Mr Hogg's, the Blue Bell, in Low Harrogate, in time for dinner.'

The last landlords were Mr and Mrs Clayton, and after the Bell closed in November 1815, Widow Clayton retired to Rose Cottage, adjoining the entrance to Valley Gardens. The accompanying drawing shows the Bell Inn at centre, probably at the time of its closure. Well Hill may be seen in the background, with the dome of the Sulphur Well temple, and part of the old Crown Inn, at right. The original Bell Inn seems to have been demolished in 1846 for the rebuilding of Royal Parade, but because the 1841 Act had prohibited the excavation of cellars within yards of the Sulphur Well, the cellars of the Bell Inn were incorporated into Royal Parade, where they again form part of the Old Bell Tavern.

In a town which is swimming with pseudo wine bars and pubs, the majority of which appear to be trying to capture to the youth market, complete with horrible canned muzak, games machines, awful bottled drinks, and other dross, it is refreshing to hear that the Old Bell Tavern has none of this, aiming rather for an adult market which values good conversation, good ale, good cooking and general conviviality.

Christmas Eve 1897

The run-up to Christmas had been unseasonably mild. Both the *Herald* and *Advertiser* had commented on October and November being warmer than April or May, and the combination of roses blooming through thick fog revealed to Harrogate's pre-Christmas shoppers that the mild weather was continuing well into December. And here was Christmas Eve, with not the faintest touch of frost, other than that which etched the glass partitions of the James Street Banks. Inside the Bradford Old Bank, the clerks looked restlessly at the great mahogany clock, ticking its way towards five o'clock, and a closing, which, on account of Christmas, management had ordained should be an early one. Not that early closing was usual, or even desirable.

The traders of Chapel Street, Beulah Street, Cambridge Street, and Parliament Street, as representatives of the town's leading shopping streets, were only just beginning to take Christmas Eve into their strides. They would remain open as long as there were customers to serve, although the really grand establishments, such as that of James Ogden, would expect to close their doors by about 7.00pm.

Further along, at the corner of Station Square, Standing's Grocery Emporium was a hive of frenzied activity. The liveried commissionaire would be opening the double glass doors for customers well up to 10pm, whilst at the rear, in Back James Street, a horde of boys were arriving and departing with pedal bikes, each of which carried a large hamper at front, and a maroon liveried advertising panel beneath, on which the legend 'Edward Standing, Grocer to the Quality ōf Harrogate, phone 26' was painted. Most of the packages carried within the hampers were of brown or dark blue paper, along with larger sacks of flour, sugar, or salt, bottles of every conceivable concoction, and tins containing Mr Edward Standing's celebrated Christmas Cakes. Larger orders had been dispatched by carriage, those destined for the far reaches of the borough boundary at South Drive, Granby Comer, or the new Kent Road, had been cleared by mid-afternoon.

Not that Mr Standing had a monopoly in his trade. Further along James Street, Gunson's had a reputation for fine pastries and the most elaborate spun sugar ever seen in Harrogate, whilst Quentin Acomb, of Oxford Terrace, was widely regarded as the Spa's leading bread maker. But Standings, with its two cafés, bakery, and wooden-floored shop, was regarded as a generally 'superior' business, and – moreover – it was the only one with the new-fangled telephone.

The tall, commanding figure of the new Town Clerk, Joseph Turner-Taylor, entered James Street from the Prospect Hotel's Garden end. Although he refused to allow any women into his office – even his fiancée was banned from those sacred quarters on top of the Victoria Baths in Crescent Gardens – he had, as a very special favour, given Ann, his fiancee, permission to meet him in the downstairs lobby at 5.00 o'clock to go Christmas Shopping. She had walked to the Victoria Baths by half-past four, and waited patiently for the arrival of her betrothed. At precisely 5pm, the Town Clerk appeared, and greeted Ann affectionately, before setting out for James Street. With his burnished top hat and heavy black overcoat, which T-T wore regardless of the temperature, but rather as a mantle of civic dignity, the Town Clerk and his wife entered the premises of Sheffield's fish restaurant, next to the Bradford Old Bank in Princes Street.

This was Ann's favourite, even though she was rather in awe of the proprietor, Alderman Sheffield, known to Harrogate as 'Fishy Joe'. Sitting himself at his regular stall, T-T eyed the nervous looking lad in attendance, clad in an enormous white apron which touched the well-scrubbed floor, and boomed: "Now then, I want a dozen oysters for me, ten for little hen here, and bring me a pint of stout – and look sharp". The stout would be brought over from Maxwell Grayson's, at the corner of Back James Street, in the special silver tankard favoured by T-T, whose companion was turning over in her head those last minute purchases and arrangements which always have to be considered in order that 'preparations' can be considered complete. And then there was that mysterious 'treat' that Joe had mentioned. What could he have meant? There was also the Christmas Eve service at St Peter's, to look forward to, when the choir would be on top form. She wondered if Joe would take his pocket book along, to note the names of those wicked Corporation employees who failed to obey his order that he expected to see 'the lot of 'em' at the municipal church service that evening. He'd have his pencil, too.

The market was a heaving mass of people by the time that the couple entered by 6pm, just as the clock – the baroness's clock, as all Harrogate called it – struck the hour. Row upon row of turkeys, chickens, geese, pheasant, widgeon and teal were strung along a series of grids, which had been run up over the frontages of the poultry dealers – above the stalls of Jonas Berry, Isaac Postlethwaite, George Robinson, John Steel, and Charlie Winterburn. Outside the market, on Station Square, the premises of Ernest J. Batchelor, florist, were being emptied, and flowers supplied from the Batchelor Hot Houses on Harlow

Hill streamed forth to grace the homes of Victoria Park, The Oval, Beech Grove, and other estates throughout the town. The most famous florist, Alva Hall, of Albert Street, who was charged with the beautification of Harrogate Station, was similarly enjoying the Christmas rush, as were his other rivals, Bonsall's of 42 Parliament Street, Bootlands, of 10 Westmoreland Street, and Gould, within the market.

The London trains continued to arrive at Harrogate Station throughout Christmas Eve, disgorging their passengers into the welcoming arms of friends, families, porters, cabmen, and coach drivers. For one of the porters, Benjamin Jobling, it all seemed a bit frantic, not at all like it used to be, back in 1847, when he had been a post boy, employed on the old Leeds to Ripon Union Coach, which rolled into Harrogate's Brunswick Hotel every Christmas Eve, to be welcomed by the landlord with hot slices of spotted dick and rum sauce, served on pewter plates, and always accompanied by a mug of hot punch. But not until the horses had been attended to.

Benjamin Jobling recalled the cry 'see to the horses, see to the horses'. Now, it was all grease, oil, coal and steam, printed timetables, and impersonal officials. Harrogate was definitely declining. Some of the arrivals were greeted by representative of the hotels – who now despised the appellation 'inn' used by old Harrogate. This was indeed a change, visitors arriving to enjoy the delights of the George, the Granby, the Queen, the Hydro and the Cairn, guests who had no thought of 'taking the waters', or any injunction other than to 'enjoy themselves'.

As the evening progressed, so the fog thickened, just as the *Herald* predicted. Having selected some special items from the market, the Joseph Turner-Taylor and his fiancee walked down Station Parade, along Bower Road, beneath the railway arch, where 'old Fred' was, as usual, turning the handle of his street piano in exchange for coppers, and crossed into Dragon Fields where, to her astonished eyes, Ann saw that a wooden pavilion theatre had been erected, before which a large poster proclaimed 'Jessup's Jinks and Jollities – special Christmas show'. So this was what Joe had meant by a 'treat'. She shared her husband's enjoyment of good, witty music hall shows, with the songs and dance routines, for which Jessup was famous.

Jessup, employed by entrepreneur Newell, was not the only showman to take advantage of the Christmas crowds. West Park, from the Prince of Wales Hotel, as far as Victoria Avenue, was alive with streams of what the conservative *Advertiser* called 'the lower orders', people who celebrated Christmas in the many taverns and beer houses which had given the area a name as bad as that of Denmark Street up at Smithy Hill. They poured out of the new public saloon behind the Prince of Wales, out of the Golden Lion, the Commercial, the Coach and Horses – just fresh from its recent rebuilding – Muckle's Vaults, and from Tower Street's many 'dives' – the Albert, the Belford, and the Coachmaker's Arms. People, in the main intent on celebrating Christmas with the mixture of cheap alcohol and mawkish sentiment which the English can make so much their own. But what matter, for it was Christmas, and good cheer was undoubtedly in the air. Later, it would be another matter, as a few of the merrymakers would be up before the magistrates for causing breaches of the peace. A group had gathered outside the Coach and Horses, attracted by a street-piano player, churning out *My Old Dutch*, which the crowd accompanied with raucous and sentimental enthusiasm.

The respectable retailers of wines and spirits were also enjoying record sales. On Station Bridge, William Riegels-Cory expected not to get to his bed before Christmas morning, although his neighbour the chemist Butterfield, had shut up shop as early as 8pm Riegels-Cory suffered from the lack of underground storage space, so he rented the cellars of the old Spa Rooms in Ripon Road, where he stored some of his wares. Fortified wines were his speciality, and he deplored the contemporary fashion for French product. His own holdings of Madeira, Ports, and Marsalas were unrivalled, as was his no-longer fashionable old 'Mountain', a favourite of Alderman Fortune, Chairman of the Bench of Magistrates and 'Father' of the Council.

As for that worthy gentleman, Alderman Fortune sat in his study at Alston House, Mount Parade, and contemplated Harrogate's progress. The new Royal Baths were proving a splendid investment, and had reinforced the town's position of 'Queen of English Watering Places' – what was Bath in comparison, with its few miserable springs. Harrogate had 88 of them, and all different. Now there was this matter of the Kursaal to resolve, and the gigantic reservoir scheme to complete – once the legal and financial niceties had been resolved at Westminster. The town could do with a proper Town Hall, and the matter of the new Theatre had to be encouraged. No doubt about it, the place was changing. It was all very different from when he was a boy, when he'd gone bird nesting for eggs among the whins of Tewit Well Stray, back before the railway viaduct crashed at Knaresborough. Then there was all this talk about new monster hotels: a Grand, a Palace and a St James. It would all have to be looked at very carefully.

Parliament Street had a forlorn gap. Dr Titus Deville's house was missing, torn down, it was said, for a new building. Dr Deville had departed, taking with him his scarlet cloak, silver buckled shoes, court-dress, and home-made liquors, to be replaced by a monstrous new shopping arcade in the gothic style. Opposite, the premises of Knowles Wine Merchants were as busy as those of Riegels-Cory on Station Bridge, Maxwell Grayson in James Street, or J. Hale & Co at the corner of Swan Road and Crescent Road. The hot mutton pie vendors did splendid business, especially when a group of carol singers entered Parliament Street from the Ginnel, having just had their best-ever takings from a half-drunken crowd in Richardson's Exchange Saloon and Billiard Rooms.

Down in Walker Road, the peace of the Royal Spa Gardens was broken by the activities of rival players of street pianos, hurdy-gurdy men, barrel-organ grinders, and assorted singers. Who were vying with each other for the attention of the public. The rival claims of this motley crew had become something of a scandal in the town, as it seemed nothing could be done about it. The racket penetrated Cheltenham Parade and Mount Parade, reaching even through the double windows of Alderman Fortune's study, causing an entry to be made on his notes for the new Stray Bill which would shortly be sent up to London: 'Street musicians – control of!'

Skipton Road divided Harrogate's richest and poorest. On the south side, at Smithy Hill, a fight had broken out inside the Denmark Tavern, between a husband and his wife, when the former good lady accused her life's companion of spending his entire weekly earnings on drink, to the neglect of herself and five children. Such brawls were not uncommon at the Denmark Tavern. Across Skipton Road, well away from the unseasonal words which were being exchanged by the tavern's clientele, Grove House presented a dazzling spectacle, being- together with its grounds – lit by owner Samson Fox's amazing invention, water gas lamps. Multi-millionaire inventor and genius Samson Fox, thrice Mayor of Harrogate, would spend a Christmas quieter than usual, as his beloved mother, Sarah Fox, was declining rapidly. No longer troubled by his tiresome lawsuit with the author of *Three Men in a Boat*, Jerome K. Jerome, Samson Fox was free to devote himself to family matters.

The present Mayor, Alderman James Chippendale, had spent most of Christmas Eve in his carriage, attended by some of his labourers, and children from the Methodist Free Church Sunday School, distributing gifts for the poor. He had visited Tower Street first, passing on to Union Street, before the public houses emptied, so that the Christian work of relieving the community's less fortunate citizens could be done in relative peace. The great cream and brown coach, drawn by two fine horses, and followed by one of his firm's heavily-laden business carts, had moved on to Smithy Hill, where a team of hand-picked volunteers were waiting to distribute some of the 136 turkeys, 146 hares, 122 pheasants and chickens, 22 stones of flour, 110 parcels of groceries and 150 packets of tea, which the Mayor hoped would provide a Merry Christmas. Some of the children came from the newly-established Boy's Brigade, others from the many Church organisations with which the town was so well endowed.

The Mayor passed through old Bilton, before the last stage of his travels, which took him to Rattle Crag and Harlow Cottages. As his carriage passed the great houses on Ripon Road and Duchy Road, the Mayor gazed with approval on the sight of many candle-lit Christmas trees, glinting through well-cleaned windows, and presenting an altogether pretty view to the passer-by. Later – much later – when the Town Clerk and his wife had been long returned from the Christmas Eve service at St Peter's, when the organ grinders had been moved on from Walker Road, and when the Salvation Army Band no longer carolled the residents of Victoria Avenue from their pitch in Victoria Circus, the Mayor returned to the town centre, passing along a James Street in which only a handful of businesses were still open, their gas-lit interiors casting a yellow, brackish light through the fog and across the damp pavements, his horses hooves clip-clopping over the exclusive street's wooden setts.

Ordering his driver to park opposite the darkened premises of George Newby, fishmonger and poulterer, Alderman Chippendale pushed open the doors of his friend's shop, where Edward Standing sat upon a chair, counting money. It was nearly midnight, and the last customers had departed some minutes before. The delivery boys had finished their rounds, and the commissionaire had enjoyed a last drink at the North Eastern Hotel before joining his family at home in Nidd Vale Terrace. On seeing the Mayor, Standing rose, and crossed the shop to greet his old friend. From the ceiling, half a dozen globes of wired, milky glass shone upon the gleaming mahogany counter which snaked round the outside of the grocery department.

As it was shop policy to block up the big windows on James Street and Station Square with fixed window displays, the inside of the shop was like an Aladdin's cave, surrounded by shelves on which were displayed thousands of cartons, bottles, tins and boxes, all containing the choicest wares. Two enormous 'island' counters displayed, on little marble stands, cakes, crystallised fruits, marzipans, and whatever a wealthy and demanding clientele demanded, along with cold meats, cheeses, butter and fruit. Sacks of biscuits, cereals, flour, and various sugars, lined the floor beneath the great mahogany counter, and in the far corner of the shop was the cashier's office, surrounded by a brass-work screen, into which a regular criss-crossing of pneumatic tubes passed, carrying cash and receipts from every quarter of the shop. "There's coffee downstairs," Standing announced to his friend, " 'appen I'll tek some," replied the Mayor.

Downstairs consisted of the smoke room, now deserted, but still warm. Sitting the Mayor at one of the old sycamore chairs, by a massive oak bench, the hot coffee was brought and consumed with evident pleasure. Surrounded by the oak panelling, the several chess sets set aside for another day's play, the two men sat. Looking at his fat pocket watch, the Mayor exclaimed: "Blimey, it's midnight – Christmas Day, 'appy Christmas, Standing." The two men toasted each other in hot coffee, as the smoke-room clock chimed midnight, in harmony with the clock within the Bradford Old Bank, and all the other clocks in Harrogate. It was Christmas Day, 1897. Merry Christmas Harrogate.

A chauffeur-driven motor car awaits a customer at Cornall's photographic studios, Station Square, *c.*1909.

Spring Grove, with the Hotel Majestic at far left, in the winter of 1907.

Another view of Prospect Terrace, *c.*1902; showing the use of parasols to protect visitors from the sun.

The junction of Devonshire Place and Westmorland Street – a good place for street games, at least in 1909!

Hookstone Road, showing Wood's Farm, and the Convent.

Cold Bath Road, *c.*1910.

A horse-drawn bus turns from Skipton Road into King's Road, *c.1914*.

The Convent of the Holy Child, Hookstone Road.